Hurricane
Katrina

Other books in the At Issue series:

Alternatives to Prisons
Anorexia
Antidepressants
Anti-Semitism
Are American Elections Fair?
Are Privacy Rights Being Violated?
Biological and Chemical Weapons
Child Labor and Sweatshops
Child Sexual Abuse
Cosmetic Surgery
Creationism Versus Evolution
Do Children Have Rights?
Does Advertising Promote Substance Abuse?
Does the Internet Benefit Society?
Does the Internet Increase the Risk of Crime?
Drug Testing
The Ethics of Abortion
The Future of the Internet
How Can Domestic Violence Be Prevented?
How Can the Poor Be Helped?
How Does Religion Influence Politics?
How Should One Cope with Death?
How Should Society Address the Needs of the Elderly?
How Should the United States Treat Prisoners in the War on
    Terror?
How Should the World Respond to Natural Disasters?
Indian Gaming
Is American Culture in Decline?
Is Islam a Religion of War or Peace?
Islam in America
Is Poverty a Serious Threat?
Is the Gap Between the Rich and Poor Growing?
Is the Mafia Still a Force in America?
Is the World Heading Toward an Energy Crisis?
Is Torture Ever Justified?
Legalizing Drugs
Managing America's Forests
Nuclear and Toxic Waste
Prescription Drugs
Protecting America's Borders
Rain Forests
Religion and Education
Responding to the AIDS Epidemic
The Right to Die
School Shootings
Steroids
What Causes Addiction?
What Is the State of Human Rights?

At ✳ Issue

Hurricane Katrina

William Dudley, *Book Editor*

Bonnie Szumski, *Publisher*
Helen Cothran, *Managing Editor*

GREENHAVEN PRESS
An imprint of Thomson Gale, a part of The Thomson Corporation

Detroit • New York • San Francisco • San Diego • New Haven, Conn.
Waterville, Maine • London • Munich

LIBRARY OF CONGRESS CATALOGING-IN-PUBLICATION DATA

Hurricane Katrina / William Dudley, book editor.
  p. cm. — (At issue)
Includes bibliographical references and index.
ISBN 0-7377-3551-1 (lib. : alk. paper) — ISBN 0-7377-3552-X (pbk. : alk. paper)
  1. Hurricane Katrina, 2005. 2. Emergency management—Gulf Coast (U.S.)
3. Disaster relief—Government policy—Gulf Coast (U.S.) I. Dudley, William,
1964– . II. At issue (San Diego, Calif.)
HV551.4G85 H36 2006
363.34'922—dc22   2005055131

Printed in the United States of America

Contents

Introduction

Hurricane Katrina, which struck Florida on August 25, 2005, and made landfall again along the Gulf Coast in Louisiana, Mississippi, and Alabama four days later, has already been declared the costliest and most destructive natural disaster in U.S. history. The hurricane's strong winds and storm surge not only resulted in the destruction of many towns and communities, but also the breakdown of the system of levees protecting the historic city of New Orleans, Louisiana, leading to widespread flooding of the city. Months later, many parts of New Orleans remained uninhabitable. Economic damages from Hurricane Katrina have been estimated at more than $200 billion. By December 2005 the official death toll of the storm had topped thirteen hundred people, with more than six thousand missing and unaccounted for. More than a million people were displaced by the storm, many of whom remained homeless months later. An estimated 120,000 homes were abandoned and will probably be destroyed in Louisiana alone. As the American people attempted to assess and react to these and other costs of Hurricane Katrina, they asked a haunting question: Were the damages of Hurricane Katrina in any way preventable?

At first glance, such a question might seem absurd. Hurricane Katrina was the result of elemental natural forces over which humanity has little control. Hurricanes are a product of weather conditions found in certain regions of the world, including the tropical regions of the North Atlantic Ocean. During hurricane season (June 1 to November 30), a combination of factors—areas of low barometric pressure, ocean waters warmed and evaporated by the sun, and Earth's rotation in space—work together to produce massive storms that are classified as tropical depressions, tropical storms, and hurricanes, depending on their size. When Katrina hit Florida on August 25, it was a relatively small hurricane that was downgraded to a tropical storm as it crossed the state, with wind speeds of less than 75 miles per hour (mph). But it gained strength when it left Florida and traveled across the warm waters of the Gulf of

Mexico, peaking with sustained winds of 175 mph and gusts of 215 mph. The storm front extended 120 miles along the Gulf Coast, created dozens of tornadoes, and generated a surge that pushed the waters of the Gulf of Mexico up to a mile inland and created twenty-foot-high waves that pounded the levees around New Orleans.

But the fact that destructive forces unleashed by Hurricane Katrina were part of a natural and (to some extent) predictable climate system makes the question of whether Katrina's damages could have been prevented—or at least minimized—all the more pointed. Hurricane Katrina was one of twenty-six storms (including thirteen hurricanes) named and tracked during the 2005 hurricane season alone. Residents of New Orleans and other communities struck by Katrina may not have known for sure that they would be affected until hours before it happened. But all knew—or should have known—that they lived in a part of the world in which hurricanes occur regularly. In 2002 the *New Orleans Times-Picayune* ran a series of articles on the hurricane threat, stating that "it's only a matter of time before South Louisiana takes a direct hit from a major hurricane" and concluding that plans for hurricane preparedness were lacking. Given that foreknowledge, it is difficult to blame the death and destruction solely on the hurricane itself. Decisions made by individuals and by U.S. society as a whole also played a role.

Questions have been raised, for example, about whether government did enough to plan mass evacuations and otherwise prepare the people of New Orleans and other communities for hurricanes. Such plans are generally the province of state and local governments, but in large disasters the U.S. president can declare a federal disaster area, enabling the federal government—specifically the Federal Emergency Management Agency (FEMA)—to step in and coordinate rescue and relief efforts. President George W. Bush did issue such a declaration for the Gulf Coast region on August 27, two days before Katrina hit the Gulf Coast. However, state, local, and federal authorities have all been criticized in the wake of Hurricane Katrina for what was seen as a slow and ineffective response that indicated a lack of planning or forethought. For example, the mayor of New Orleans called for a mandatory evacuation on the morning of August 28. However, little was done to organize public transportation for people who did not own cars. FEMA officials also came under criticism for failing to bring enough resources to affected areas and for being seemingly unaware of some of the humanitarian crises created by Katrina. Many people both in and outside of New Orleans were left to fend for themselves without food, water, power, medical supplies, or police protection. It took several days for National Guard troops to come into New Orleans and begin to restore order. In an open letter to President George W. Bush, the editors of the *Times-Picayune* stated: "We're angry, Mr. President. . . . Our people deserved rescuing. Many who could have been were not. That's to the government's shame."

An even more basic question raised by Hurricane Katrina involves the decision to develop and populate America's Gulf Coast region. Despite the risk of hurricanes, many Americans seek to build homes with an ocean view. The coastal population as a whole in the United States increased 28 percent between 1980 and 2003, leaving many more people in hurricane-vulnerable zones. In addition, many economic activities in the region, such as dredging canals, drilling for oil and gas, and constructing offshore casinos, have damaged or destroyed thousands of acres of the area's natural wetlands. Over the past century an estimated million acres of marshland and coastal islands in Louisiana alone have been replaced by open water. These land forms have historically acted as a sponge to absorb the wind energy and flooding of hurricanes; their absence may help explain why the damage created by Hurricane Katrina was far greater than that wrought by Hurricane Betsy, which struck New Orleans in 1965 at a time when more square miles of wetlands protected the city. One of the most devastated areas, St. Bernard Parish near New Orleans, lay just south of a two-hundred-meter-wide canal that was constructed through dense swampland in the 1960s; critics believe that the canal acted as a "hurricane highway" that contributed to the flooding of the community and the deaths of more than one hundred people.

The problem of wetlands loss has been compounded by a specific aspect of coastal development that has undergone renewed scrutiny following Hurricane Katrina: the complex, decades-old system of earthworks, floodwalls, pumps, and levees that have channeled the Mississippi River and have kept the city of New Orleans—much of which exists below sea level—from flooding. This system has prevented the Mississippi River from replenishing coastal wetlands and barrier islands with natural sediment as it has in previous centuries. But it also has protected New Orleans from floods—at least until

Hurricane Katrina, when the system failed in several key places. Some have argued that a New Orleans flood was inevitable given its location, but investigators have attempted to ascertain whether the Hurricane Katrina flooding may instead have been the result of structural and design flaws and local mismanagement of the levees.

The question of whether Hurricane Katrina's devastation could have been at least partially prevented by human preparedness will affect the many decisions to be made about the region's future. Questions raised about the lack of preparedness revealed by Katrina will affect future efforts by FEMA and state governments to plan for natural disasters. Questions raised about the role of wetlands in absorbing hurricanes have stimulated debate on whether to restore them, even if it means not repopulating New Orleans and other communities to pre-Katrina levels. In the immediate weeks after Hurricane Katrina, Congress appropriated $62 billion for hurricane relief aid. But whether residents and businesses will rebuild commercial structures, roads, houses, and schools in Katrina-affected areas may depend on whether more federal aid will be available to rebuild the levee system to withstand the strongest hurricanes.

1

Hurricane Katrina Revealed America's Lack of Natural Disaster Preparedness

Paul C. Light

Paul C. Light is a senior fellow in governance studies at the Brookings Institution and the author of The Four Pillars of High Performance.

The response to Hurricane Katrina was marred by disorganization and confusion. It showed that the United States remains unprepared for both natural disasters and acts of terrorism. The United States must spend more time and money to build a better response system that can anticipate disasters, attract and deploy a talented workforce, and provide both central coordination and local flexibility to disaster relief efforts.

Even as the Gulf Coast states battle to recover from Hurricane Katrina, Washington should take heed of the chaos surrounding the early relief effort. If this is what happens when the nation has two days of advance warning, imagine the aftermath of a surprise attack using a chemical, biological or nuclear device.

Katrina underscores the urgent need to build a robust national preparedness and response system. There will be plenty of stories of heroism in coming months as thousands of volunteers descend on the disaster zone. But the hubris is already showing. Thousands of residents ignored the evacuation warnings; many relief agencies waited until the hurricane had passed to start sending supplies and volunteers to jumping-off points in surrounding states; and the president was heading to California as the hurricane moved in. Although the Department of Homeland Security [DHS] and its Federal Emergency Management Agency are moving at near-light speed to coordinate an unprecedented relief effort built around DHS's National Response Plan, the nation must get even faster in the future.

Ironically, a Category 5 hurricane was already on the Department of Homeland Security's list of 15 planning scenarios for emergency response. In an effort to give organizations more specific guidance about how to plan for catastrophic events, the department issued the scenarios last winter [2004–2005] in the hopes that governments, businesses and charitable organizations would start rehearsing their response.

> *Katrina underscores the urgent need to build a robust national preparedness and response system.*

Unfortunately, a yet-to-be-released survey by New York University suggests that most Americans expect disaster to hit just about anywhere but home. Most have enough canned goods and bottled water in the closet to last a few days, but they want their local police and fire agencies, the Red Cross, and charities to tell them what to do in the event of a catastrophe. The problem with Katrina is that many citizens did not listen before the hurricane, and communications were cut off after. Plenty of emergency planners had nightmares about a Category 5 hurricane hitting somewhere, but few woke up and started preparing.

Katrina underscores the urgent need to build a robust national preparedness and response system that can bend and flex to the unique circumstances of natural or human-caused catastrophes. Based on my analysis of hundreds of high-performing organizations identified by the nonpartisan Rand Corp., such a system must be alert to impending catastrophe, agile in implementing well-designed plans for response and recovery, adaptive to surprise events such as the collapse of the New Orleans levees, and aligned so that everyone can pull together, from Washington on down to the initial first-responder who shows up at the site of a disaster.

The Four Pillars of an Effective System

Here are the four pillars of a robust response system:

- *Alertness to what lies ahead.* As Katrina surely suggests, the nation faces many possible catastrophes, some that can be predicted, others unexpected but inevitable. A high-performing response system is constantly scanning a wide range of scenarios while establishing signposts that will trigger the kind of action that would have saved precious time after Katrina had moved on. Katrina gave fair warning, but no terrorist will.

- *Agility in recruiting, training, retaining and redeploying a talented, flexible workforce.* Too many local governments have yet to complete even the most basic training on how to respond to a small-scale catastrophe such as a terrorist bombing at a local shopping center, let alone an attack on a chemical refinery. Even when governments, businesses, and charitable organizations think ahead, they rarely do so together, creating a sum less than the parts when catastrophe strikes. Agility also involves making sure first responders can talk to each other on equipment that can survive a major catastrophe.

- *Adaptability.* Although no one can be prepared for every eventuality, a robust system provides enough flexibility in dollars, equipment and 3,000-pound sandbags to bring innovation to bear on unexpected events such as flooding and massive fatalities. Unfortunately, Congress, the president and many governments have been doing homeland security on the cheap or through pork-barrel spending.

- *Alignment of all organizations to a central plan.* As New Orleans Mayor Ray Nagin complained the day after his levees collapsed, there are "way too many fricking . . . cooks in the kitchen." Having an aligned system means just one cook in the kitchen and hundreds of servers on the front lines. If aligning a system means that governments, businesses and charitable organizations have to cede authority to a single director, so be it. Catastrophe is no time for protecting bureaucratic turf.

Creating this kind of robust response system requires time, money, constant rehearsal and concentration. And it requires individual organizations that are robust, too. This is why Homeland Security Secretary Michael Chertoff's recently proposed reorganization is so important to implement. By eliminating needless layers of management and focusing on the most likely scenarios, Chertoff is taking an essential step toward creating a more robust department, which in turn will help create a more robust response system.

If Congress really wants to prepare for future disasters like Katrina, it will attach Chertoff's reforms to whatever relief legislation it is sure to pass in coming weeks. At least in planning for catastrophe, preparedness starts at the top, not the bottom, with clear signals about where to invest, whom to engage and how to coordinate.

2

Hurricane Katrina Revealed America's Social and Economic Inequalities

Walter Ellis

Walter Ellis writes for The Spectator, *a British journal.*

Hurricane Katrina revealed how the American people continue to be divided by race and class. New Orleans, the city hardest hit by the storm, is one of the poorest cities in the United States; flood victims there were predominantly poor and black. The United States is lacking the necessary political leadership to unite the country and overcome its economic and social divisions in the wake of the hurricane's destruction.

It is tempting when looking back on natural catastrophes to see them as symbols of the affected nation's fatal departure from good sense or moral progress. Hubris is retrospectively invoked to justify the evident nemesis. The horrific events in New Orleans and surrounding territories are being picked apart, like entrails in aboriginal Africa, as though there might be a clue, even a message, that will explain how America has begun to fall apart.

In a bid to pre-empt at least some of Congress's investigative zeal, the President announced on Monday [September 6, 2005,] that he would carry out his own inquiry into the catastrophe, but senators and congressmen refuse to be deterred

Walter Ellis, "The Grim Lessons of Hurricane Katrina," *The Spectator*, September 10, 2005, pp. 14–16. Copyright © 2005 by *The Spectator*. Reproduced by permission.

and are to launch their own investigation. One thing that is certain is that no one will emerge from the audit with much credit; certainly not the state and municipal authorities, who have shown themselves to be whining incompetents. Much of the sniping at Bush has been infantile. Critics have depicted the President as uncaring, callous, even racist, which those who know him or have worked with him will recognise as risible. Far harder to rebut, however, will be the charge that he and his advisers failed to heed the central lesson of 11 September 2001: that danger can strike at any time from any quarter and the nation must be prepared. Plan B is all very well, but there has to be a Plan A.

> *It is tempting when looking back on natural catastrophes to see them as symbols of the affected nation's fatal departure from good sense or moral progress.*

Since 9/11 the administration has abandoned the tradition of deferring to local authorities in cases of disaster. Under the National Response Plan of 2004 the federal government pre-empts local and state government in its responsibility to act when there is 'any natural or man-made incident, including terrorism, that results in extraordinary levels of mass casualties, damage, or disruption severely affecting the population, infra-structure, environment, economy, national morale, and/or government functions.' Hurricane Katrina was the test of that doctrine, and by any reasonable reckoning the administration failed the test.

Poverty in America

New Orleans is one of the poorest cities in the Union. Half the households have an income of less than $22,000; nearly 30 per cent of the population lives officially in poverty; and it has one of the worst violent crime rates in America. Nearly two thirds of the population are black, and most of those live in the areas worst affected by flooding. Katrina opened the floodgates not just to the waters that poured in, but to resentments that had built up over many years. Violent criminals, also black, were freed to operate without restraint. They robbed and raped with impunity. Some, out of a kind of madness, even took to firing on their rescuers, provoking a deadly response from the tardy National Guard. But for thousands of others, looting was less an opportunity than a necessity. Shops and stores became open invitations to people who had struggled for years and now found themselves at the mercy of the elements, abandoned and forgotten by the authorities. This was *Lord of the Flies* on a metropolitan, even an operatic scale. For Americans outside the stricken area, it was as if the slimy underside of their national life and character had suddenly been exposed. They were embarrassed and ashamed by what happened in New Orleans.

But similar deprivation exists in Detroit and St Louis, as well as in large sections of New York, Chicago, Philadelphia and Los Angeles. For nearly half of the people of the United States, these are hard times. The gap between the haves and have-nots has widened to almost Third World dimensions over the past 30 years. The rich and successful have flourished, but the middle classes are in trouble, saddled with debt and uncertainty (to say nothing of college fees), while many Hispanics barely scrape a living. Factories have been closing at an alarming rate, with much of the slack being taken up by China, whose power in the world America is only now beginning to appreciate. Unemployment in August [2005] stood at 5 per cent (10 per cent for blacks). Of the 132 million non-farm jobs, only 14.3 million were in manufacturing. Forty million Americans cannot afford health insurance, and the number is growing. In New York, health premiums rose by more than a quarter during the first half of the year, adding to the sense of crisis. Over the same period, for every two additional cents paid to low-paid workers, 50 cents extra went to top earners.

> *For Americans outside the stricken area, it was as if the slimy underside of their national life and character had suddenly been exposed.*

Positive discrimination may be on the way out, but for millions of black children the idea of going to college was always unreal. Their schools had prepared them for a lifetime of welfare dependency and petty crime, not study. White trailer trash fared little better. They weren't even allowed to kick blacks around any more. And Hispanics? Well, they were the people who cut your grass, picked your oranges or delivered your groceries.

A Fraying National Unity

The flag was supposed to be what held these disparate groups together. Underneath, no matter what, everyone was an American. The terrorist attacks of 2001 appeared at first to reinforce the sense of shared citizenship. There was pride in adversity and a determination to take the fight to the enemy. But economic difficulties, high unemployment, a declining dollar and the cost of the war in Iraq began to eat away at the ties that bind.

While proclaiming itself the champion of freedom, ready to spread democracy throughout an often unwilling world, America turned in on itself, endlessly debating who and what it stood for. Equal under God Americans may have been, but equal in the sight of Washington apparently they were not. The poor made up the overwhelming majority of the armed forces, just as they were 90 per cent of those trapped in the Gulf State floods. No senator's son wore uniform in Iraq.

It's looking bad for Bush. Republicans such as Senator Chuck Hagel are calling for troops to be pulled out of Iraq. . . . Referring to the handling of the New Orleans crisis, another Republican senator, Susan Collins, said bluntly, 'Government at all levels failed.' Announcing that the Senate governmental affairs committee would hold hearings, she added, 'It is difficult to understand the lack of preparedness and the ineffective initial response to a disaster that had been predicted for years, and for which specific, dire warnings had been given for days.'

Political Fallout

No one can say for sure what the long-term political fallout will be from the intertwining crises of Iraq and Katrina, but the President's approval rating fell last month [August 2005] to a record low of 45 per cent, hit not only by the continuing quagmire in Iraq but by spiralling gas prices—and this was *before* Katrina struck. Although he will not be standing for re-election, Bush has more than three years of his remit left to run and must be seen to assist his party's cause as it heads towards the increasingly uncertain mid-term congressional elections.

On the Democrat side, the assumption has to be that Bush's

danger is a liberal opportunity. It's an ill wind that blows no good. But the record of the opposition party has been dismal in recent years. Even members of the Black Caucus, indignant that so many of the dead and bereaved in New Orleans are African-American, have so far been muted in their criticism. They appear to believe that nothing can be done until the Republican establishment runs out of steam and collapses of exhaustion and its own ineptitude.

> *The destruction of New Orleans is not a symbol of the apocalypse. The situation is not yet irrecoverable.*

Too many people in politics these days, just like many of those in industry and commerce, seem to be in business mainly on their own account. Shorn of the moral exigencies of the New Deal and the Great Society, the Democrats' endorsement of tax cuts has reached the point where they have no idea how they would raise money to pay for their half-baked reforms of welfare, education and health provision. Liberalism has come to mean little more, in ideological terms, than tolerance of gays, acceptance (up to a point) of abortion and a more relaxed attitude towards religion and the death penalty. It has little to do with a new vision for America, still less the smack of firm government.

The American Right, meanwhile, is lost in denial. It denies that its invasion of Iraq was at best muddle-headed; it denies that poverty is stalking the nation and that the emergence of de facto apartheid (as in New Orleans) has resulted in the cultural Balkanisation of the Republic. Much of the denying is done by George Bush and his White House entourage, but there are echoes up and down the country. When I lived in rural Connecticut, I was struck by how little ordinary Americans knew about what was happening in the world. What they really cared about was gas prices, jobs and country music. How did they feel about the Iraq war? They liked it. It was a chance for the US to 'kick ass'. And how do they feel about it now? They hate all the dying—especially of Americans in uniform—but they'll hang on in there, at least until Bush finds some way to bring the boys home 'with honour' (i.e., not with their tails between their legs).

With America in such turmoil at home and abroad, what hope is there that trust can be restored between government and people? It used to be widely accepted that a reformist Democrat government had to be followed by a 'sensible' Republican administration. The one stood for the underdog, the other for competence, old-fashioned values and patriotism. Today the view is that Democrats are too frightened, spineless and self-serving to make any difference, while Republicans are thought to have lost any sense of rectitude. Both parties favour consensus in smoke-free rooms to the vagaries of conflict.

A Lack of Leadership

It is the tragedy of contemporary America. The greatest nation on earth has stopped going forward, except with bayonets fixed. The frontier, once mystical, now begins at every citizen's front door. Where it used to be the duty of Americans to help their neighbour, today it is to build an investment portfolio. Mum, Dad and the kids are all that's left of the commonwealth. The emblematic power (as distinct from the reality) of the family has become the touchstone of political rhetoric, allowing the state to step back and claim that if you can't stand on your own two feet, ain't no one else gonna do it for you. Not that the generous instincts of ordinary 'folks' have died completely. Americans gave generously to nations hit by last winter's [2004] tsunami (though less generously per capita than Europeans). In the aftermath of Hurricane Katrina, they have once again reached for their cheque books. But it is too little too late.

The destruction of New Orleans is not a symbol of the apocalypse. The situation is not yet irrecoverable. But it's broke and someone has to fix it. An inspirational leader, of either party, who can take the country by the scruff of the neck and mobilise its resources in defence of traditional values and responsible government is needed.

Sadly, what we will probably get instead is Hillary Clinton —Mrs Bubba. After the hard nuts, the fudge.

3

The Media Exaggerated Aspects of the Hurricane Katrina Disaster

Dan Gainor

Dan Gainor is a journalist and former managing editor with Congressional Quarterly. *He directs the Media Research Center's Free Market Project, an operation that seeks to improve media coverage of America's system of free enterprise.*

In the hours and days after Hurricane Katrina hit, the media retold numerous lurid tales involving anarchy and crime in the city of New Orleans. Most of these stories were unfounded rumors that turned out to be untrue. These false stories have done lasting damage to America's reputation abroad and raise questions about the objectivity and reliability of the mass media.

After the levees broke in New Orleans, the city appeared to descend into chaos before our eyes. Americans sat in front of their TVs, watching Katrina's flooding and hearing tales of horror. On Sept. 2 [2005] ABC's "Good Morning America" described New Orleans "as the city spirals out of control." Charles Gibson continued: "There appears to be anarchy. Reports of rapes, riots, fires, bodies in the street."

That was how much of the media depicted New Orleans—a city lost to anarchy. Only it wasn't true.

There is no doubt that Katrina was an incredible tragedy, but it was nowhere near what was reported. What is true is that the sloppy coverage of Katrina's devastation will leave its mark

Dan Gainor, "Politicians, Media Combine to Create Disastrous Coverage," *San Diego Union-Tribune*, October 2, 2005. Copyright © 2005 by Dan Gainor. Reproduced by permission.

on the media and on America for years to come.

This past week [prior to October 3, 2005], the New Orleans *Times-Picayune* led the parade of media that did their best to set the record straight about what really happened. They told a story of epic failure, but they weren't writing more stories blaming the Katrina disaster on FEMA [Federal Emergency Management Agency] or President Bush. These told of the failure of local officials and media who got the story wrong, giving new meaning to the term "bad news." The Sept. 25 *Times-Picayune* story painted a new picture: "[T]he vast majority of reported atrocities committed by refugees—mass murders, rapes and beatings—have turned out to be false . . ." That's not what we were told, over and over again.

> **"** *State and local officials . . . didn't stamp out the sparks of rumor—they spread them like arsonists.* **"**

For weeks, the media dumped blame on FEMA, President Bush and the rest of the federal government for conditions worthy of a war zone. In a Sept. 12 cover story, *Newsweek* included this ironic comment: "How the system failed is a tangled story—" Actually, it was countless tangled stories—news stories.

The very structure of news reporting contributed to the disaster because news often focuses on the unusual or outlandish. In a crisis, almost everything is unusual or outlandish. With Katrina, journalists had no way to cope with the fact that many of the people they interviewed were distraught and spouting rumors. And there is no true accountability now that those reports have been proven false.

Relying on Politicians

Journalists are taught to count on elected officials for much of their information, especially the kind needed during a crisis. Thus, the media turned to Louisiana politicians and police for crime statistics, the death toll and for rational commentary to offset rumors.

But state and local officials from Louisiana's governor on down didn't stamp out the sparks of rumor—they spread them like arsonists. Democratic New Orleans Mayor C. Ray Nagin claimed on the Sept. 5 "Today" show that "it wouldn't be unreasonable to have 10,000 [dead]." A month after the storm, the Louisiana death toll stands at 896.

> *Media critics on the left and right have skewered Katrina coverage.*

Certainly, crimes occurred. Officials now say 14 people died between the Convention Center and the Superdome, after seemingly endless accounts claiming far worse. Only one or two of those were reportedly homicides.

Nagin and New Orleans Police Chief Eddie Compass took their act to the "Oprah Winfrey Show" with even more outrageous claims that remain unproven. Nagin told of evacuees trapped in the Superdome "watching dead bodies, watching hooligans killing people, raping people." Compass, who has since resigned, went even further with his claim that "We had babies in there. Babies getting raped." No one has been able to match the tabloid TV extravaganza that Oprah put on. Oprah cried "No, no, no, no," while Compass told of the horrors that allegedly went on in the dome—horrors officials now deny.

And Oprah milked it for all it was worth, interviewing traumatized people without ever taking into account that they were exhausted, drained, angry and scared. To prey on them was bad enough. To embrace rumor was irresponsible.

Counting on Journalists

Journalism is supposed to be a first draft of history. In the days that followed Katrina, the media reported it like it was the script for "Fear Factor." Given the behavior of the politicians on the scene, it's almost hard to blame the media. But they didn't just rely on officials. Journalists hit the streets, eager for a story too sensational to watch from the sidelines.

With communications and 911 out, reporters turned to second-hand or third-hand reports. The Sept. 11 broadcast of CNN's "American Morning" relied on actor James Caviezel. Caviezel, best known for his work as Jesus in the "The Passion of the Christ," told how he met an 82-year-old woman who claimed she "watched three men rape an 11-year-old girl, watched a man walk up and shoot a police officer right in the head."

Rather than question it, CNN's Miles O'Brien simply said, "What a horrific thing to endure." O'Brien joined the ranks of journalists who set aside their natural skepticism and reported almost any outlandish claim they could find. Most never reminded viewers that it takes time to sort out the truth in such a terrible disaster.

Media critics on the left and the right have skewered Katrina coverage. Liberal groups complained that racism made it easy for reporters to accept the idea of a predominantly black city turning to anarchy. Journalists, who had attacked President Bush about race only weeks before, found themselves uncomfortably coping with their own attitudes. On September 13, CNN's Soledad O'Brien took a typical media position and asked, "Was the administration slow to respond when pictures of mostly black people were on TV, and over days, were clearly in dire straits?" Will she now critique her own co-workers with equal vigor?

Conservative critics saw Katrina as yet another media attempt to discredit Bush and Republicans. The media didn't create the hurricane, but reporters seized the opportunity to portray the president as racist and out of touch. We know the first draft of history was rough indeed, but it's too late to change that traumatic impression. The damage to Bush's popularity has been done—with false information.

Could It Happen Again?

The aftermath of the hurricane hasn't just shaken our faith in government; it's shaken our faith in our nation, our politicians and our media. Worse still, it has become part of the world's myths about America. In a day when news from other nations is just a click away, millions saw the misreporting repeated endlessly. Even Britain's respected *Financial Times* described the "rape and the lawlessness that overwhelmed New Orleans" in its Sept. 8 issue. That will continue to undermine U.S. efforts around the globe, though the stories remain untrue.

Several major news organizations followed the *Times-Picayune* report . . . trying to correct the record. That is impossible. The story journalists told of rape, murder, and mayhem has oozed into our culture. It will forever be another urban legend.

The media were right about a key aspect of Katrina: The system did break down. Politicians made a bad situation worse and the media's 24-7 news cycle piled rumor after rumor on top of that. The media spend every day demanding accountability from politicians, businesspeople and everyone they encounter. Now that they are having a rockslide in their own glass house, who is there to call them on it? The bigger question is: Could we have another journalistic catastrophe like this again? The unfortunate answer is, probably yes.

4

Hurricane Katrina Revealed Management Problems of FEMA

Elaine Karmack

Elaine Karmack teaches at Harvard University's John F. Kennedy School of Government. She served as a senior policy adviser to former vice president Al Gore during the administration of President Bill Clinton. She created and managed the National Performance Review, a White House policy council that audited the performance of the federal government and proposed various management reforms.

The dismal response to Hurricane Katrina by the federal government, including the Federal Emergency Management Agency (FEMA), was in part caused by management decisions of the administration of President George W. Bush. Under Bush, FEMA was placed within the new Department of Homeland Security, and natural disaster planning was shunted aside in favor of planning for terrorist attacks. Furthermore, reforms initiated by former president Bill Clinton and vice president Al Gore to reduce bureaucratic red tape and empower frontline workers to cope with crises were reversed under Bush, leaving the government less able to respond quickly to Hurricane Katrina.

There is a widespread consensus that something "went wrong" in the government's response to Hurricane Katrina. In the first weeks, the Bush administration was clearly anxious to pin the blame on the Democratic governor of Louisiana and the Democratic mayor of New Orleans. But even the president has now taken some responsibility. The departure of Federal Emergency Management Agency (FEMA) Director Michael Brown,[1] in an administration that is more inclined to give out medals to people who preside over failures than to fire them, is as close as we will get to an admission that "something" at the federal level went wrong.

So what was it? How did we get to the point where bureaucracy got in the way of saving lives? Is it simply the incompetence of a former Arabian Horse Association executive [Brown] in the wrong job at the wrong time? Or can we find explanations in the management philosophy of the White House?

Company Management Philosophies

Management philosophies tend to be non-partisan, which is why they so rarely attract press or public attention. A former colleague of mine in the Clinton administration has compared the Clinton-Gore management agenda to the Bush management agenda. According to John Kamensky, now at IBM, there are some similarities. The Bush administration, for example, continued to focus on measuring the results of government programs that began in the Clinton administration, including the emphasis on e-government.

> **Putting FEMA into the Homeland Security Department took the agency backward.**

But there are differences in management philosophy, too. Once a full investigation into the response to Katrina is under way, these differences may turn out to have had significant effects. For instance, during the Clinton administration, Vice President Al Gore, who ran the federal government's management-reform efforts—or "reinventing government," as it was called—constantly emphasized empowering front-line federal employees so that they could do their jobs with a minimum of red tape. This philosophy was not very popular with their bosses in the civil service, nor with their political ones, but it was fre-

1. Brown resigned his post on September 12, 2005.

quently reinforced by the vice president himself and by the reinventing-government team. It involved, among other things, working with the federal unions that represent many front-line workers in order to get them to help us figure out what was really taking place on the ground.

> **_FEMA officials waited for signatures and orders while people died._**

In contrast, the Bush administration has centralized its reform efforts and pushed unions to the side. In so doing, it sent a powerful message to its front-line workers: Don't take any initiative or you might end up in trouble. The result? Story after story like the one from Dan Wessel, owner of a transportation company with a contract to move supplies who didn't get the green light from FEMA until it was too late. Aid from around America and from around the world was offered in a timely manner, but no one was empowered to get it there. In news story after news story, FEMA officials have been fingered as the people deferred to red tape and, in so doing, turned down timely help.

The FEMA job is to manage a large and diverse network of helping agencies. As Kamensky and others have pointed out, managing networks is a fundamentally different exercise than managing a top-down bureaucracy and yet, in the early crucial hours, too many people were sticking to nonsensical protocols or saying "no" when they should have been "getting to yes."

The Evolution of FEMA

How did FEMA lose its ability to manage the multiple sources of help that it had traditionally managed? The major fault lies with the decision to fold FEMA into the new Department of Homeland Security. Many, myself included, advised against this. Those of us who worked on the reinventing-government team had seen the transformation of FEMA, which began in 1993 with President Clinton's appointment of James Lee Witt. Under him, FEMA went from an agency that Congress wanted to abolish to an agency that worked. The fundamental concept in Witt's turnaround of the agency was the "all hazards" approach. Underlying it was the realization that regardless of cause—earthquake, hurricane, tornado—there were similarities in disaster response that could be planned for.

Putting FEMA into the Homeland Security Department took the agency backward. Not only did it bury what was once a freestanding agency in a new and unwieldy bureaucracy, but the decision erased the lessons from the 1990s that had allowed FEMA to serve the country so well. FEMA went from all hazards to one hazard: terrorism. Its traditional mission—helping states and localities prevent natural disasters and prepare for them—was pushed aside.

In the end the story will be less about how *much* money was spent and more about how it was spent. In one example, local officials complained that once FEMA's grant-making authority to state and local governments had been centralized in the Homeland Security Department, you could get money for protective chemical suits but not for flood control.

Failing to Follow the Plan

FEMA officials waited for signatures and orders while people died. Finally, however, fault lies with the failure of this White House to understand the implications of its own post-September 11 disaster planning. The first four paragraphs on page 44 of the National Response Plan, adopted in December of 2004, make it perfectly clear that standard procedures regarding federal, state, and local operations can be expedited or ignored if lives are at stake in a catastrophic event. The plan itself anticipated the New Orleans situation, where police officers and other first responders were stuck on rooftops saving their own families and frequently unable to get to their jobs. And yet Justice Department lawyers argued about the use of military force and FEMA officials waited for signatures and orders while people died.

Hurricanes, earthquakes, and terrorists will always end up killing people. But bureaucracy should not. That's the lesson from Hurricane Katrina. Let's hope it is learned before the next disaster.

5

Hurricane Katrina Revealed the Ineffectiveness of Big Government

David Boaz

David Boaz is the executive vice president of the Cato Institute, a libertarian think tank, and author of Libertarianism: A Primer.

Government at all levels—federal, state, and local—failed in responding to Hurricane Katrina. Government officials failed to adequately plan for the hurricane, failed to spend enough money on levees and flood control, and failed to deliver disaster relief in a timely manner or to maintain order following the hurricane. The private sector, including churches, charities, volunteers, and corporations, did a better job in delivering hurricane relief than the government, despite interference from government bureaucrats. The lesson of Hurricane Katrina is not to give government more money and power, but to keep government limited and focused.

You've got to hand it to the advocates of big government. They're never embarrassed by the failures of government. On the contrary, the state's every malfunction is declared a reason to give government more money and more power.

Take Hurricane Katrina, a colossal failure of government at every level—federal, state, and local. Thirteen days after the

David Boaz, "Catastrophe in Big Easy Demonstrates Big Government's Failure," *Cato Daily Commentary,* September 19, 2005. Copyright © 2005 by the Cato Institute. All rights reserved. Reproduced by permission.

hurricane, the Sunday *Washington Post* blared, "The Steady Buildup to a City's Chaos/Confusion Reigned at Every Level of Government."

And what's the response of the big-government crowd? "The era of small government is over." "It's libertarianism, more than anything else, that has transformed [New Orleans] into an immense morgue." "Americans living along the Gulf Coast have now reaped the consequences of that hostility . . . to the role of government as a force for good."

> *Government was sluggish in responding to the disaster.*

Let's look at the facts. Government failed to plan. Government spent $50 billion a year on homeland security without, apparently, preparing itself to deal with a widely predicted natural disaster. Government was sluggish in responding to the disaster. Government kept individuals, businesses, and charities from responding as quickly as they wanted. And at the deepest level, government so destroyed wealth and self-reliance in the people of New Orleans that they were unable to fend for themselves in a crisis.

And some people conclude that we have too little government?

A Failure to Plan

Start with the failure to plan. As Paul Krugman wrote on September 2 [2005]:

> Before 9/11 the Federal Emergency Management Agency [FEMA] listed the three most likely catastrophic disasters facing America: a terrorist attack on New York, a major earthquake in San Francisco and a hurricane strike on New Orleans. "The New Orleans hurricane scenario," *The Houston Chronicle* wrote in December 2001, "may be the deadliest of all." It described a potential catastrophe very much like the one now happening.

The warning was there. And after 9/11, federal spending on homeland security skyrocketed, up to about $50 billion in the current fiscal year [2005]. A Department of Homeland Security [DHS] was created, with FEMA folded into it. Meetings were held, memos were written, 190,000 employees went on the DHS payroll, billions were spent. If the FEMA memo and the *Houston Chronicle* article weren't enough, the *New Orleans Times-Picayune* published a five-part series in 2002 titled "Washing Away." So federal, state, and local governments were prepared for Katrina, right?

Wrong. During the Bush administration, Louisiana received far more money for Army Corps of Engineers civil projects than any other state, but it wasn't spent on levees or flood control. Surprisingly enough, it was spent for unrelated projects favored by Louisiana's congressional delegation.

State and Local Government Failures

What about the state and local governments? If you're going to have a city below sea level in hurricane country, you'd better have some disaster plans. And plans they had. But apparently those plans didn't include strengthening the levees or evacuating residents.

> *As the storm hit New Orleans with full force, the local government effectively abdicated.*

After Katrina left a path of destruction in Florida and picked up steam over the Gulf of Mexico, Governor Kathleen Babineaux Blanco conferred emergency powers upon herself. So she knew disaster was coming, not that that seemed to matter. Her Department of Homeland Security refused permission for the Red Cross and the Salvation Army to go into the city and deliver water, food, medicine, and other relief supplies to those suffering at the Superdome and convention center. Similarly, she took several days to sign a simple proclamation allowing doctors licensed out of state to help the sick and injured. Several doctors sat around for days waiting to go to work. As the storm hit New Orleans with full force, the local government effectively abdicated. Reports of looting began only hours after the assault.

FEMA issued a sternly worded release on August 29, the same day the hurricane made landfall along the Gulf Coast, titled "First Responders Urged Not to Respond to Hurricane Impact Areas." FEMA wanted all the responders to be coordinated and to come when they were called. And that was one plan they followed. As the *New York Times* reported September 5:

> When Wal-Mart sent three trailer trucks loaded with water, FEMA officials turned them away, [Jefferson Parish president Aaron Broussard] said. Agency workers prevented the Coast Guard from delivering 1,000 gallons of diesel fuel, and on Saturday they cut the parish's emergency communications line, leading the sheriff to restore it and post armed guards to protect it from FEMA, Mr. Broussard said.

Those weren't the only examples. The city declined Amtrak's offer to carry evacuees out of the city before the storm. On September 2, the *South Florida Sun-Sentinel* reported, "Up to 500 Florida airboat pilots have volunteered to rescue Hurricane Katrina survivors, transport relief workers and ferry supplies. But they aren't being allowed in." Hundreds of firefighters responding to a call for help were held in Atlanta by FEMA for several days of training on community relations and sexual harassment.

Even President Bush acknowledged September 13 that "all levels of government" failed to respond adequately to the most-anticipated natural disaster in history. But the government failure in this instance runs deeper.

> **Before and after Hurricane Katrina, businesses and charities responded effectively.**

Who were the people who suffered most from Hurricane Katrina? The poorest residents of New Orleans, many of them on welfare—the very people the government has lured into decades of dependency. The welfare state has taught generations of poor people to look to government for everything—housing, food, money. Their sense of responsibility and self-reliance had atrophied. When government failed, they had few resources to fall back on.

Some journalists have suggested that the despair of poor New Orleanians undermines President Bush's case for the "ownership society." In fact, the suffering visible in the poorest parts of the city is a perfect example of the failure of the "non-ownership society." People had become trapped in dependency, with neither financial nor moral assets to rely on.

Private Relief Efforts

Meanwhile, despite FEMA's best efforts, immediately after the hurricane the private sector—businesses, churches, charities, and individuals—began to supply services to the victims. Within 10 days after the catastrophe, charities had raised $739 million, far ahead of the pace of donations after the 9/11 attacks or the Asian tsunami. Experts predict that donations might eventually exceed the $2.2 billion donated after 9/11.

Even though private companies have no obligation for disaster relief, they started planning for a Katrina response before the hurricane made landfall. Two *Washington Post* reporters wrote that it's "unsettling but inescapable" that commerce resumes quickly after natural disasters, that "Wal-Mart and Home Depot are in a class by themselves, going to extraordinary lengths to keep their customers supplied." Would they really prefer that Wal-Mart and Home Depot closed in honor of the victims? Surely it was better for the survivors that these companies planned for disaster and reopened their stores rapidly.

Wal-Mart's emergency preparedness division had ordered 10,000 seven-gallon water jugs for hurricane season. A full week before Katrina hit New Orleans, Wal-Mart ordered 40,000 more. Jefferson Parish president Broussard said that "if American government would have responded like Wal-Mart has responded, we wouldn't be in this crisis."

Drug companies created their own distribution systems to move medicines and medical devices into the storm-ravaged areas. Ten days after the storm the U.S. pharmaceutical industry had donated cash and products worth $42.5 million.

Churches and charities in the area and as far away as New Mexico and Maryland began sending trucks loaded with food and clothing and offering homes to evacuees. The *Washington Post* reported that "owing to stealthy acts of hospitality that are largely invisible to government"—and fortunately so, lest the government try to shut down these uncoordinated efforts—"hundreds of thousands of people displaced by Hurricane Katrina seem to be disappearing—into the embrace of their extended families."

That's nothing new. After Hurricane Andrew in 1992 the government set up tent cities, which went largely unused as people were taken in by family, friends, church members, and neighbors.

Government Should Be Limited

Faced with yet another failure of government to plan or respond adequately, a surprising number of people want to transfer more money and power from the private sector to government. After colossal disasters, politicians have two or three typical responses. They visit the stricken area; throw money at the problem—Congress has approved $62 billion in emergency aid so far for the ravaged areas; and usually add a new layer of bureaucracy to existing government agencies. After 9/11, Congress created the Department of Homeland Security. Could adding "and Natural Disasters" to the department's title be far behind?

Coincidentally, Congress passed a second, $51.8 billion relief bill on the same day the Associated Press released a study of where the $5 billion small-business relief money after 9/11 went. It found that the funds went to a South Dakota country radio station, a Virgin Islands perfume shop, a Utah drug boutique, and more than 100 Dunkin' Donuts and Subway shops—"companies far removed from the devastation." Fewer than 11 percent of the loans went to companies in New York and Washington.

But it's no accident that governments often fail at their tasks. The incentives are all wrong. Profit-seeking companies are constantly driven to innovate, improve, cut costs, and deliver better service for less money, lest they lose customers to their competitors or even go out of business. Churches and charities are motivated by love and commitment, as well as by the need to satisfy donors or run out of money. Governments can raise taxes or print money. If a government agency fails at its mission, the usual response is to give it more money next year—not a very good incentive for success. Politicians would rather cut a ribbon at a Cowgirl Hall of Fame than fix potholes or levees.

Before and after Hurricane Katrina, businesses and charities responded effectively. Government failed at even its most basic task of protecting lives and property from criminals. When massive and bloated governments at all levels disappoint, the solution is not to give them more money. Rather, the solution lies in a government limited in scope and ambition, and focused on its essential functions.

6

Hurricane Katrina Revealed the Problems of Conservative Antigovernment Ideology

Tom Vilsack

Tom Vilsack is the governor of Iowa. He chairs the Demo-cratic Leadership Council (DLC), an organization that seeks to stimulate debate within the Democratic Party about pol-icy issues.

Government is the instrument by which people under-take responsibilities that cannot be done by individuals. These responsibilities include protecting people from natural disasters like Hurricane Katrina and helping communities recover from such crises. However, con-servatives who control the national government have long harbored hostility or indifference to government programs and have placed political operatives in key government positions. Hurricane Katrina should re-mind Americans of the importance of an effective and responsive national government and the limited ability of private charities to deal with both natural catastro-phes and ongoing social problems.

The people of the Gulf Coast (following Hurricane Katrina) have shown tremendous strength and resilience in the face of incredible adversity. Amidst the suffering and death, and the destruction of so many homes and dreams, we have witnessed

Tom Vilsack, "Statement of DLC Chairman Governor Tom Vilsack," September 15, 2005, www.dlc.org.

extraordinary examples of individual strength, courage and generosity.

We have also witnessed a vast outpouring of sympathy, material and personal support, and solidarity with the victims of Hurricane Katrina across our land. It's been a heartening reminder that we are, in fact, a national community, and not simply a collection of disconnected individuals or groups.

An Incompetent Government Response

But at the same time, our national community has been diminished by the inadequate and sometimes incompetent response of one of its essential elements, our national government.

Let me be clear: government is not the embodiment of our sense of community; but [neither] can you have a strong, united and effective community without it. Government is nothing more nor less than the instrument whereby our people come together to undertake collectively the responsibilities we cannot discharge alone. It can and must reflect our values, further our aspirations, and most of all, defend our common safety and security without favor, and with constant attention to the most vulnerable among us.

These observations may seem obvious to most Americans, but unfortunately, they are not obvious to many in power in Washington today. The failures in our national response to Hurricane Katrina did not simply stem from mistakes, however egregious, of individuals whose replacement with more experienced and competent public servants will take care of the problem in the immediate and distant future. These failures represent the broader failure of an ideology of contempt for the responsibilities of government, and for the sense of community that is fundamental to genuine self-government.

Conservative Ideologues

All too often, conservative ideologues who now honeycomb the halls of our great public buildings in Washington have promoted the idea that government is an alien institution that illegitimately confiscates and redistributes resources to no great purpose other than sustaining our armed forces at the absolute minimum of effectiveness. These ideologues have viewed government, even the federal government they control from top to bottom, as a necessary evil to be tolerated, an

38

obstacle to be overcome and undermined, a "beast" to be starved. And worse yet, when their plans to dismantle government are thwarted, they tend, not surprisingly, to view federal agencies as little more than a vast patronage opportunity for fellow-partisans who don't much believe in the missions they are supposedly pledged to perform.

This ideology explains how a vital public entity like FEMA [Federal Emergency Management Agency], a model of responsive government just a few years ago, became what insiders call a "turkey farm," a holding pen for political operatives needing employment between campaigns.

> *The failures in our national response to Hurricane Katrina . . . represent the broader failure of an ideology of contempt for the responsibilities of government.*

And this ideology explains why the administration's opposition to retaining some civil service protections in the Department of Homeland Security—an opposition couched in claims that Democrats were risking our national security—appears to have been motivated in part by a desire to accommodate political appointees with few qualifications.

If this mix of hostility and indifference towards government's positive role in our national community had brought us a cheaper and leaner federal government, it might have served some positive purpose. But as we all know, the federal government has become fatter and meaner instead. We are learning every day that there really is something worse than a big, debt-ridden government that tries to do too much and fails. It's a big, debt-ridden government that tries to do too little, and succeeds.

An Opportunity to Rethink Our Attitude

That's why the devastation and human tragedy of Hurricane Katrina provides a painful but necessary opportunity for us all to rethink our attitude towards our own public institutions and those who serve in them, rejecting the false choice of government as an end in itself and government as a dead end remote from our worthier endeavors.

And that's why current Republican proposals to turn the Gulf Coast into a conservative ideological laboratory with private-school vouchers, wholesale deregulation, and suspension of wage standards on federally financed construction projects must be rejected. A second, ideologically driven abandonment of public responsibility in this region would be intolerable.

What Hurricane Katrina Should Teach Us

Katrina should convince us that the federal budget is not just a year-end ledger of government's largesse, but an agenda of collective responsibilities so important that we choose to tax ourselves to discharge them.

Katrina should remind us that levees, water treatment systems, wetlands restoration projects, and environmental protection efforts are not useless "pork" or "red tape," but essential investments—yes, investments as rational and cost-effective as any made by private businesses—in the safety and prosperity of our people.

Katrina should compel us to acknowledge that entrenched poverty and discrimination remain important and morally central subjects for public policymaking, not simply objects of private charity.

And most of all, Katrina, by calling forth our community's best values of solidarity and shared sacrifice, should inspire us to demand a government attuned to those same values, providing "opportunity for all and special privileges for none."

The first words of our Constitution read: "We, the people of the United States, in order to form a more perfect union. . . ." This is our government, the chosen instrument of our national community, and it's time we held it to the same standards we hold for ourselves and each other as free and self-governing citizens. If Katrina makes that possible, all the suffering and the sacrifice may not be in vain.

7

Racism Played a Part in America's Response to Katrina

DeWayne Wickham

DeWayne Wickham writes a weekly column for USA Today.

Televised images of New Orleans following Hurricane Katrina revealed that many of the victims stranded in the flooded city were both poor and black. For many people this raised the question of what role their poverty versus their skin color played in their plight. Both race and class played a role in the fate of poor blacks victimized by Hurricane Katrina and the government's poor response. However, racism was a more dominant factor. While the disaster overwhelmingly affected the poor, in New Orleans the poor are mostly black people who have been forced into poverty by a racist society.

It wasn't long after the tortured images of thousands of black men, women and children holed up in the Louisiana Superdome and Morial Convention Center started appearing on TV newscasts that talk of an old conundrum surfaced.

Was it the color of their skin or their place in society that made the suffering among that city's blacks so great? The race or class question pits those who believe that racism is the root cause of much that ails blacks against those who say it is their economic and social condition that is the problem.

More often than not, the answer splits along predictable fault lines. Many liberals—especially blacks—see racism as the culprit. Conservatives, by and large, think it's the lifestyle choices of poor blacks that lock them into the underclass.

I think it's a combination of both. But as with most mixtures, one is more dominant than the other.

Actions of Survival

Anyone who saw the television footage of black looters hauling away appliances and TV sets is right to believe that the criminal behavior of some blacks has more to do with the hand life deals them than does the color of their skin.

But to view the mindless acts of a few thugs in the same way as the taking of food and drink by the larger body of blacks misses an important distinction. The vast majority of blacks were simply trying to survive—a struggle that was impacted more by race than by class.

> *Blacks lived in neighborhoods that were hardest hit by the flooding.*

Before Hurricane Katrina struck, New Orleans' population was 67% black, but a whopping 84% of the city's poor were black. Many whites lived in neighborhoods at the highest elevations. Most blacks lived in the lower-lying areas of the city. According to *The New York Times,* 35% of black households in New Orleans didn't own a car. In other words, blacks lived in neighborhoods that were hardest hit by the flooding—and were less likely to have an automobile to escape.

In New Orleans, as in much of the rest of this country, race defines class. It was the poor in New Orleans who had the most difficulty evacuating. It was the poor who were forced to resort to looting to feed themselves and their families while being left stranded by the incompetence of government officials. It was the poor who made up the bulk of those who were housed for days in the Superdome and convention center without much food, water, medical help or police protection. And most of the poor in New Orleans are black.

Poverty is the new Jim Crow. It is a subtler—but no less hurtful form of racism. Last year [2004], a quarter of all blacks in this country lived below the poverty level, compared with less than

9% of whites. The South, where the majority of blacks live, is the nation's poorest region. That's not a chance relationship.

Reasons for Poverty

"For a variety of well-documented reasons, poverty is disproportionately experienced among minorities," writes Michael Stoll, a UCLA professor for Public Policy, in a paper he will present . . . at a "Colors of Poverty" conference sponsored by the University of Michigan.

Stoll says there is a relationship between where people live and their level of poverty. Poverty is higher in central cities than in suburbs. "Location," he says, influences the access people have to "good schools, decent housing, crime-free neighborhoods, productive contacts and other benefits that help shape, determine or constrain access to opportunity."

If that sounds as if Stoll thinks "class" is to blame for what happened to poor blacks in New Orleans, you're wrong. "If you press me, I have to say that race played more of a role in how fast" the government came to the aid of that city's blacks, he told me.

I couldn't agree more.

8

Racism Is Not Evident in America's Response to Katrina

John Leo

John Leo is a columnist for U.S. News & World Report.

Claims that racism had something to do with problems in the government's response to Hurricane Katrina are wrong. Those who argue otherwise are painting a false picture of a racist America. The media, by recycling such arguments, is harming the nation. Government problems following Katrina are best explained by simple incompetence that hurt white victims as well as black.

A letter to the editor of the *Oregonian,* in Portland, Ore., said of Katrina: "I am deeply disturbed and angered by the number of reports claiming racism has something to do with the delay in the relief effort. These claims are unsubstantiated and a complete lie. To even suggest that our government would allow people to die simply because of the color of their skin is despicable. . . . In a time of national crisis, another media-driven race war is the last thing this country needs."

Amen to that. The usual racemongers played their usual role. Jesse Jackson said the scene in New Orleans "looked like Africans in the hull of a slave ship." Carol Moseley Braun, the former Democratic senator from Illinois, said the scene in New Orleans was similar to the fatal neglect of blacks after Reconstruction. Morning show hosts at a New York City rap station detected "genocide" in New Orleans. On a slightly more respectable level, black members of Congress, judges, and activists stoked racial polarization. "This is a racial story," said an attorney for the National Association for the Advancement of Colored People. A black judge in Arkansas said Katrina revealed the "ugly, stinking, pus-filled sores" of racism.

> *The hard-hit mostly white parishes around New Orleans waited just as long as the poorest wards of the city did for help.*

A common charge was that aid would have come more quickly if New Orleans had been predominantly white. There is no evidence for this at all. Across-the-board incompetence at every level of government is a far more compelling explanation than racist intent or behavior. The hard-hit mostly white parishes around New Orleans waited just as long as the poorest wards of the city did for help.

Double Standard

Evidence-free assertion of racism seemed everywhere. Robert Parham of the Baptist Center for Ethics in Nashville said Katrina "disclosed our racism in multiple ways," none of which he bothered to mention. The most poisonous statements were the ones linking failure in New Orleans to racist violence of the past. "You'd have to go back to slavery, or the burning of black towns, to find a comparable event that has affected black people this way," said University of California-Los Angeles sociologist and African-American studies Prof. Darnell Hunt, thus positioning the disaster in New Orleans as similar to some of the worst racism in history. This kind of rhetoric has an effect. Two thirds of blacks polled say they see racism as a cause of the failures to cope quickly with Katrina.

The mainstream media played a role, too. Several TV anchors and interviewers prodded or invited black officials to say they spotted heavy racism in New Orleans. Comedian Nancy Giles, on CBS *Sunday Morning,* announced that Katrina victims went without food and water for days simply because they were black.

Racial charges were endlessly recycled. Rapper Kanye West's claim that "George Bush doesn't care about black people" has been published more than 400,000 times, according to a Google search. Almost as famous are the captions of similar photos of a white man "finding food" in New Orleans and a black man "looting." The captions were taken everywhere as evidence of racism. An editor in Kenya thought they were.

The looting caption may have been unfair, but the constant citing of it merely reflects resentment of racism without presenting any real evidence of racist behavior.

The *Washington Post* ran a Page 1 story, "To Me, It Just Seems Like Black People Are Marked." The story was basically harmless, but the headline probably did some damage, confirming for many readers that blacks have been singled out for unfair treatment.

An essay on Katrina in the *Post* Style section used campus diversity jargon referring to blacks as "the Other," saying, "Mainstream America too often demonizes the Other because, well, we've been conditioned to do so." No explanation of why mainstream America, so woefully conditioned and addicted to demonizing, has donated over $750 million to mostly black hurricane victims.

Two Visions of America

Heather MacDonald writes on the *City Journal* website, "That people are giving so feverishly in spite of the competing images of looting by the flood victims and the reports of murder and rape is even stronger proof that racism has lost its grip on the American mind: The givers are refusing the bigot's reaction of impugning an entire race by the loathsome behavior of a few."

The media have been reporting on two tracks. One stresses the empathy and generosity of mainstream America, as reflected in the astonishing donations, the thousands of volunteers who poured into the area, the collection and shipping of tons of food and clothing, and the extraordinary efforts made by rescuers, often at the risk of their own lives. The other features the usual bitter denunciations of racist America. Which do you suppose is a better indication of where the nation wants to go?

9

Hurricane Katrina Offers America an Opportunity to End Its Racial Divide

Carol Moseley Braun

Carol Moseley Braun served as a U.S. senator from Illinois from 1993 to 1999. She later served as a U.S. ambassador to New Zealand and Samoa.

America has a long history of racism against black people, and racism may have played a part in the slow response to Hurricane Katrina. But open racism is no longer acceptable, and most Americans are sympathetic to hurricane victims regardless of race. These changing attitudes may enable Hurricane Katrina to be a catalyst for a renewed national effort against poverty and homelessness and a turning point in healing America's ongoing racial divisions.

Years ago, I was "adopted" by the Rhodes family of New Orleans following a fateful boat ride on the Mississippi River shared with Joan and Sandra Rhodes and Mary Landrieu, now a senator from Louisiana. Mr. Rhodes, the patriarch of a sprawling, active family would joke with me that Chicago, my hometown, was "New Orleans' backyard" and that the connection between our cities was more than just a railroad, but was a spiritual, tribal one.

My own family had long ago left the city and taken the fabled ride on the train they called the City of New Orleans, arriving in Chicago at the turn of the last century, determined to escape the crushing racism that even the gaiety of the French Quarter could not disguise.

The Rhodes' family businesses started even earlier, during the backlash against Reconstruction, when rampaging whites pillaged, lynched and raped any unfortunate black they might encounter. The history books are vague about how many people died, but the riots were of such ferocity that blacks from the surrounding parishes fled for safety to New Orleans. Bodies of the victims piled up, and as there had been no mortuary service for blacks, the first DuPlain Rhodes collected them in his buggy and gave them a proper burial—no small feat in a city built below sea level. And so began the Rhodes Funeral Company that is still in business today.

Racism and Hurricane Katrina

The Rhodes' business has to operate at capacity now, in the wake of Hurricane Katrina and the stunning failure of government to provide for the welfare of the people. No one knows yet how many people have died in Louisiana or Mississippi, but everyone knows that the death toll is tragic and horrendous. Those who survive will have stories no less chilling than the stories passed down the generations from survivors who fled the night riders in the late 1800s. The failure this time of the government to respond will be seen as symptomatic of the same kind of fatal neglect that made post-Reconstruction a time of infamy in U.S. history.

> *No rational person sincerely believes our government would have had such a laissez-faire attitude if the majority of the population had not been poor and black.*

The common denominator between tragedies may almost certainly be found in the nuances and realities of race, class and poverty. Assumptions were made in government that can only be explained in context of the demographics most affected by the hurricane. No rational person sincerely believes our government would have had such a laissez-faire attitude if the majority of the population had not been poor and black. No provisions were made to avert disaster. No thought was given to how people without cars or money could leave.

> *Our response to this tragedy could herald the healing of the racial divide.*

Ironically, race, racism and racial attitudes will also figure prominently in what happens now. The Republican speaker of the House, Dennis Hastert, suggests that New Orleans should not be rebuilt and that a new city be put in a location less vulnerable to the elements. In spite of the howls about the obvious insensitivity of his remarks, he has expressed a view held by many, from architects to environmentalists. Those of us who cherish the romance and history of New Orleans will fight to rebuild it where it was, only better, and will work to assure that the destitute who are now homeless will have a chance to save their communities and own their own homes.

Tackling America's Original Sin

And so, once again, we are presented with a chance to tackle America's original sin—racism—in the aftermath of what can only be either stunning governmental incompetence or shocking discrimination. The difference, this time, is that the heart of the people has been touched by this tragedy in ways unknown a century ago. Not even the most rabid right-wing talk show hosts dare express anything other than sympathy for the suffering, the dead and dying. This generation of Americans is ashamed of racism, and in this we are of one mind: The people of New Orleans are Americans who deserved better.

The whole country is invested in creating a new New Orleans. It will never be the same again, but neither will we. Our response to this tragedy could herald the healing of the racial divide, the ending of homelessness and the beginning of a genuine effort to eradicate poverty in this country, the richest in the world.

The neglect of our homeland, the pandering to selfishness, the antipathy toward community that has dominated our national conversation has just given us a harvest no one wants to claim.

A Chance to Improve New Orleans and America

America need not have the poverty, the slums, the disease, the desperation that we have allowed to fester. Out of this tragedy could come policy initiatives to give the working poor a stake in the economy, and housing assistance that will give families a chance to own a home. The physical reconstruction can give the children schools with electrical systems that will support computer technology, with roofs and windows that are up to the challenge of the southern climate. New Orleans, one of our country's oldest cities, can be the city on a hill that invigorates the rebuilding of America.

The breakdown of government in the face of this disaster has given us all a glimpse of what could happen anywhere in America. The people in New Orleans' backyard pray for its speedy recovery, but also for the rest of our country. May we never again suffer so ugly a tear in our national fabric.

10

Hurricane Katrina Revealed the Seriousness of the Global Warming Problem

Ross Gelbspan

*Ross Gelbspan is a retired journalist. He has written numerous articles and two books—*The Heat Is On *and* Boiling Point—*on climate change and global warming.*

Global warming—created in part by the use of carbon fuels like coal and petroleum—has contributed to rising sea levels and stronger tropical storms. Hurricane Katrina is a harbinger of what global warming might bring in the future. However, the U.S. government under President George W. Bush has both failed to plan for hurricanes like Katrina and worked against cooperative global efforts to reduce the use of carbon fuels.

As floodwaters recede and bodies emerge, Americans are belatedly making some terrible connections about the [President George W.] Bush administration, which has a contempt for public planning matched only by its habit of subordinating reality to public relations. . . .

The Hurricane Katrina disaster is also a curtain-raiser for the largest-ever challenge to public planning: the consequences of global warming. If the present complacency continues, we will see more flooding, more breakdown of democratic civil order, more loss of human life and dignity, and more vivid divisions between rich and poor. . . .

A Failure to Prepare

Our latest national tragedy has been widely predicted for decades. With even a modest degree of planning, its impacts could have been drastically minimized. For years the U.S. Army Corps of Engineers has warned that New Orleans could not withstand anything more than a relatively weak (Category 3) hurricane. Ten years ago, when an intense rainstorm killed six people in the city, the corps asked Congress to provide the $430 million it had authorized to shore up levees and pumping stations. Little of that money ever materialized.

Last year (2004), *The* (New Orleans) *Times-Picayune* reported that the Corps of Engineers had determined that the Bush administration was spending less than 20 percent of what was needed to complete the fortification of the city's levees. While the massive destruction of Katrina left Americans in shock, it should have been no surprise to the federal government. In 2001, the Federal Emergency Management Agency cited a hurricane strike on New Orleans as one of the three most likely U.S. disasters. Nevertheless, by 2004 the Bush administration had cut funding to the corps' New Orleans district by more than 80 percent, as Sidney Blumenthal reported in a *Salon* article.

Earlier this year [2005], the Louisiana congressional delegation got Congress to provide about $60 million for flood protection for the city. But the Bush administration reduced that figure to $10.4 million, according to Newhouse News Service.

> *New Orleans—like . . . other low-lying population centers around the world—is especially vulnerable to hurricanes.*

While the Bush administration was cutting funding to strengthen protective dikes and levees, the state's bipartisan congressional delegation was also working to secure money for the restoration of its coastal wetlands to buffer the impacts of storm surges. Louisiana officials estimated this effort could cost

$14 billion, but the lawmakers managed to secure only a tiny fraction—$570 million over four years, according to *The Times-Picayune*. The requested multiyear, $14 billion appropriation was all but erased from the administration's energy bill. So in order to save in the short term for disaster prevention, the administration's lack of planning has yielded what will likely top $100 billion in damages—and most of it uninsured.

Rising Sea Levels

Ominously, the most massive casualty of the Bush administration's studied aversion to planning still lies in the future. New Orleans—like the Netherlands, south Florida, coastal Bangladesh, and other low-lying population centers around the world—is especially vulnerable to hurricanes, intense storms, and sea surges. In contrast to New Orleans, the Dutch have created an elaborate system of canals, dikes, seawalls, and pumps to protect the Netherlands from extreme flooding. To the Dutch—and and to most of the rest of the world—the increasing likelihood of devastating natural events constitutes an irrefutable mandate for planning.

> *One consequence of the heating of this planet is that tropical storms have become 50-percent more intense.*

Sea levels have been rising twice as quickly over the last 10 years as they were during the previous century, according to recent measurements by NASA [National Aeronautics and Space Administration] satellites. That rise is propelled more or less equally by a steady infusion of water from melting glaciers and icecaps and by the thermal expansion of the oceans themselves (as water heats, it expands).

All of this is attributable to the rising levels of heat-trapping carbon dioxide in our atmosphere, which catches heat traditionally radiated back into space. Those atmospheric carbon levels, which had stabilized at about 280 parts per million (ppm) for 10,000 years, have risen, since the Industrial Revolution, to 380 ppm—a level this planet has not experienced for at least 420,000 years—as our burning of coal and oil has accelerated.

As a result, the planet's historical temperature equilibrium has been thrown out of balance, with the earth becoming a net importer of heat. "There can no longer be genuine doubt that human-made gases are the dominant cause of [global] warming. This energy imbalance is the 'smoking gun' we have been looking for," said NASA's James Hansen, one author of the "heat balance" study published this spring [2005] in the journal *Science*.

Global Warming and Stronger Storms

One consequence of the heating of the planet is that tropical storms have become 50-percent more intense over the past 30 years, according to Professor Kerry Emanuel of MIT [Massachusetts Institute of Technology]. That increase is due to ocean warming and the resulting changes in wind patterns. While global warming doesn't increase the number of hurricanes, it makes them markedly stronger as ocean surface temperatures rise, because warming water provides the fuel for the storms.

When Katrina glanced off south Florida, it was a Category 1 storm, with wind speeds of about 70 miles per hour. But when it moved across the superheated Gulf of Mexico, with surface temperatures exceeding 80 degrees Fahrenheit, it swelled into a 170-mile-per-hour megastorm before making landfall east of New Orleans.

> **It has become overwhelmingly apparent that climate change is accelerating faster than scientists had anticipated.**

Regrettably, President Bush's anti-planning propensity seems immune to the physical changes overtaking the planet. When the Environmental Protection Agency (EPA) listed the potential impacts of climate change in the United States on its Web site in a document known as "The National Assessment on Climate Change," the White House ordered the EPA to remove or alter all references to the dangers of global warming. The president dismissed the meticulously researched document, which took four years to prepare and review, as a frivolous "product of bureaucracy." In fact, it represents the findings of more than 2,000 scientists from 100 countries reporting to the United Nations in what is the largest and most rigorously peer-reviewed scientific collaboration in history.

The Kyoto Protocol

The findings of that scientific body, the Intergovernmental Panel on Climate Change, gave rise in 1997 to an international plan to help our climate stabilize. The plan, known as the Kyoto Protocol, was signed by then-President Bill Clinton but never ratified by the U.S. Senate. In its first iteration, the protocol called on the world's industrial nations to curb carbon emissions—by some 7 percent below 1990 levels—by 2012. One of Bush's first acts as president was to withdraw America from the Kyoto Protocol.

In the last few years, it has become overwhelmingly apparent that climate change is accelerating faster than scientists had anticipated even a decade ago. As a result, the delegates to the Kyoto Protocol (which has now been ratified by more than 150 nations) are planning to speed up the timetable and ramp up the emissions-reduction goals dramatically—unless the Bush administration succeeds in scuttling the entire process.

In response to the scientific consensus finding that humanity needs to reduce its use of carbon fuels by 70 percent in a very short time, the Netherlands is already implementing a plan to curb emissions by 80 percent in 40 years. [Prime Minister] Tony Blair has committed Britain to carbon cuts of 60 percent in 50 years. Germany has vowed a 50-percent reduction in 50 years. . . . French President Jacques Chirac called on the entire industrial world to cut emissions by 75 percent by 2050.

Sabotaging the United Nations

By contrast, the response of the Bush administration has been to take dead aim at the United Nations as the world's coordinating agency on climate change. Shortly after Paul Wolfowitz was installed as director of the World Bank, he declared that the institution would make climate change a priority, promising massive investments in new coal technology. (Coal, with the heaviest carbon concentration of all fuels, is the most potent contributor to global warming of all fossil fuels.)

Following a year of secret negotiations, Bush then announced a pact with Australia, the world's largest coal exporter, and several other countries to develop "clean coal." This purely voluntary agreement not only contradicts the binding goals of the Kyoto Protocol; it also ignores the fact that one cannot clean the carbon out of coal. No matter how much coal is "cleaned," it will continue to fuel the warming of the planet.

Finally, of course, the president appointed as our new ambassador to the United Nations one John Bolton, a diplomat who has been consistently antagonistic to much of the UN's body's work. Because a more aggressive UN-sponsored Kyoto Protocol does not fit the president's preconceived agenda, his strategy boils down to sabotaging the authority of the United Nations in the area of climate change.

To the president, this sounds like a plan. To the rest of us, it seems a fast track to climate hell.

11

Hurricane Katrina Had Nothing to Do with Global Warming

James K. Glassman

James K. Glassman is a resident scholar at the American Enterprise Institute, a conservative public policy think tank, and a syndicated columnist on economic, financial, and political topics.

Environmental extremists are exploiting the tragedy of Hurricane Katrina by wrongly blaming global warming for the storm in order to promote their agenda of reducing energy consumption. There is no scientific evidence that hurricane intensity is increasing or that man-made greenhouse gases are contributing to global warming.

A profound tragedy is unfolding in New Orleans, the most beautiful city in America, with the richest cultural history and the most wonderful style of living. I lived in New Orleans for seven years. I was married there. My children were born there. I have many friends there.

My daughter, her husband and their little baby managed to get out of the city ahead of the flood on Sunday [August 28, 2005], driving 14 hours into Texas with the few belongings they could stuff into their car. They have no idea what has become of their house and their possessions, not to mention their friends, their pets, their jobs, their way of life.

Tragedies happen, and my daughter and her family are

James K. Glassman, "Katrina and Disgusting Exploitation," *Tech Central Station*, August 31, 2005. Copyright © 2005 *Tech Central Station*, www.techcentralstation.com. Reproduced by permission.

happy just to be alive. Their losses and those of hundreds of thousands of other innocents deserve mourning, prayer and respect.

Immense Forces of Nature

That is why the response of environmental extremists fills me with what only can be called disgust. They have decided to exploit the death and devastation to win support for the failed Kyoto Protocol, which requires massive cutbacks in energy use to reduce, by a few tenths of a degree, surface warming projected 100 years from now.

> *Katrina has nothing to do with global warming. Nothing.*

Katrina has nothing to do with global warming. Nothing. It has everything to do with the immense forces of nature that have been unleashed many, many times before and the inability of humans, even the most brilliant engineers, to tame these forces.

Giant hurricanes are rare, but they are not new. And they are not increasing. To the contrary. Just go to the website of the National Hurricane Center and check out a table that lists hurricanes by category and decade. The peak for major hurricanes (categories 3,4,5) came in the decades of the 1930s, 1940s and 1950s, when such storms averaged 9 per decade. In the 1960s, there were 6 such storms; in the 1970s, 4; in the 1980s, 5; in the 1990s, 5; and for 2001–04, there were 3. Category 4 and 5 storms were also more prevalent in the past than they are now. As for Category 5 storms, there have been only three since the 1850s: in the decades of the 1930s, 1960s and 1990s.

What Environmentalists Are Saying

But that doesn't stop an enviro-predator like Robert F. Kennedy Jr. from writing on the Huffingtonpost website: "Now we are all learning what it's like to reap the whirlwind of fossil fuel dependence which [Mississippi governor Haley] Barbour and his cronies have encouraged. Our destructive addiction has given us a catastrophic war in the Middle East and now Katrina is giving our nation a glimpse of the climate chaos we are bequeathing our children."

Or consider Jurgen Tritten, Germany's environmental minister, in an op-ed in the *Frankfurter Rundschau*. He wrote (according to a translation prepared for me): "By neglecting environmental protection, America's president shuts his eyes to the economic and human damage that natural catastrophes like Katrina inflict on his country and the world's economy."

The bright side of Katrina, concludes Tritten, is that it will force President Bush to face facts. "When reason finally pays a visit to climate-polluter headquarters, the international community has to be prepared to hand America a worked-out proposal for the future of international climate protection."

He goes on, "There is only one possible route of action. Greenhouse gases have to be radically reduced, and it has to happen worldwide." In other words, thanks to Katrina, we'll finally get Kyoto enforced. (He might start at home, by the way. Europe is not anywhere close to reducing CO_2 to Kyoto standards. In fact, the U.S. is doing much better than many Kyoto ratifiers.)

> *Environmental extremists do not want to be bothered with the facts.*

Ross Gelbspan, in a particularly egregious, almost giddy piece in the *Boston Globe* that was reprinted in the *International Herald Tribune*, wrote that the hurricane was "nicknamed Katrina by the National Weather Service, [but] its real name was global warming." He also finds global warming responsible for droughts in the Midwest, strong winds in Scandinavia and heavy rain in Dubai. The reason for all this devastation, of course, is that the Bush Administration is controlled by coal and oil interests.

And the *Independent*, a widely read British newspaper, reported . . . that "Sir David King, the British Government's chief scientific adviser, has warned that global warming may be responsible for the devastation reaped by Hurricane Katrina." King contended that "the increased intensity of hurricanes is associated with global warming."

No Scientific Evidence of a Link

The Kyoto advocates point to warmer ocean temperatures, but they ought to read their own favorite newspaper, *The New York Times,* which reported yesterday [August 30, 2005]:

> Because hurricanes form over warm ocean water, it is easy to assume that the recent rise in their number and ferocity is because of global warming. But that is not the case, scientists say. Instead, the severity of hurricane seasons changes with cycles of temperatures of several decades in the Atlantic Ocean. The recent onslaught "is very much natural," said William M. Gray, a professor of atmospheric science at Colorado State University who issues forecasts for the hurricane season.

An article on TCS [Tech Central Station Web site] quoted Gray last year [2004] as saying that, while some groups and individuals say that hurricane activity lately "may be in some way related to the effects of increased man-made greenhouse gases such as carbon dioxide, . . . there is no reasonable scientific way that such an interpretation . . . can be made."

Indeed, there is no evidence that hurricanes are intensifying anyway. For the North Atlantic as a whole, according to the United Nations Environment Programme of the World Meteorological Organization: "Reliable data . . . since the 1940s indicate that the peak strength of the strongest hurricanes has not changed, and the mean maximum intensity of all hurricanes has decreased."

Yes, *decreased.*

Not only has the intensity of hurricanes fallen, but, as George H. Taylor, the state climatologist of Oregon has pointed out, so has the frequency of hailstorms in the U.S. and cyclones throughout the world.

But environmental extremists do not want to be bothered with the facts. Nor do they wish to mourn the destruction and death wreaked on a glorious city. To their everlasting shame, they would rather distort and exploit.

12

The Federal Government Should Help Hurricane Victims and Rebuild Destroyed Communities

George W. Bush

George W. Bush is president of the United States.

Hurricane Katrina has uprooted and left homeless hundreds of thousands of people. The national government must do what it takes to help people rebuild their homes and to restore the areas hardest hit by the storm, including the city of New Orleans. The United States also has a responsibility to help confront the poverty-related problems made evident in Hurricane Katrina's aftermath. The hurricane has shown the generosity of the American people, and by working together the communities of the Gulf Coast can be made better than they were.

Good evening. I'm speaking to you from the city of New Orleans, nearly empty, still partly under water, and waiting for life and hope to return. Eastward from Lake Pontchartrain, across the Mississippi coast, to Alabama into Florida, millions of lives were changed in a day by a cruel and wasteful storm.

In the aftermath, we have seen fellow citizens left stunned and uprooted, searching for loved ones, and grieving for the dead, and looking for meaning in a tragedy that seems so blind

George W. Bush, address to the nation, New Orleans, Louisiana, September 15, 2005.

and random. We've also witnessed the kind of desperation no citizen of this great and generous nation should ever have to know—fellow Americans calling out for food and water, vulnerable people left at the mercy of criminals who had no mercy, and the bodies of the dead lying uncovered and untended in the street.

Stories of Generosity and Heroism

These days of sorrow and outrage have also been marked by acts of courage and kindness that make all Americans proud. Coast Guard and other personnel rescued tens of thousands of people from flooded neighborhoods. Religious congregations and families have welcomed strangers as brothers and sisters and neighbors. In the community of Chalmette, when two men tried to break into a home, the owner invited them to stay—and took in 15 other people who had no place to go. At Tulane Hospital for Children, doctors and nurses did not eat for days so patients could have food, and eventually carried the patients on their backs up eight flights of stairs to helicopters.

Many first responders were victims themselves, wounded healers, with a sense of duty greater than their own suffering. When I met Steve Scott of the Biloxi Fire Department, he and his colleagues were conducting a house-to-house search for survivors. Steve told me this: "I lost my house and I lost my cars, but I still got my family . . . and I still got my spirit."

> There is no way to imagine America without New Orleans, and this great city will rise again.

Across the Gulf Coast, among people who have lost much, and suffered much, and given to the limit of their power, we are seeing that same spirit—a core of strength that survives all hurt, a faith in God no storm can take away, and a powerful American determination to clear the ruins and build better than before.

Tonight so many victims of the hurricane and the flood are far from home and friends and familiar things. You need to know that our whole nation cares about you, and in the journey ahead you're not alone. To all who carry a burden of loss, I extend the deepest sympathy of our country. To every person who has served and sacrificed in this emergency, I offer the gratitude of our country. And tonight I also offer this pledge of the American people: Throughout the area hit by the hurricane, we will do what it takes, we will stay as long as it takes, to help citizens rebuild their communities and their lives. And all who question the future of the Crescent City need to know there is no way to imagine America without New Orleans, and this great city will rise again.

The work of rescue is largely finished; the work of recovery is moving forward.

Recovery and Rebuilding

In the task of recovery and rebuilding, some of the hardest work is still ahead, and it will require the creative skill and generosity of a united country.

Our first commitment is to meet the immediate needs of those who had to flee their homes and leave all their possessions behind. For these Americans, every night brings uncertainty, every day requires new courage, and in the months to come will bring more than their fair share of struggles. . . .

Our second commitment is to help the citizens of the Gulf Coast to overcome this disaster, put their lives back together, and rebuild their communities. Along this coast, for mile after mile, the wind and water swept the land clean. In Mississippi, many thousands of houses were damaged or destroyed. In New Orleans and surrounding parishes, more than a quarter-million houses are no longer safe to live in. Hundreds of thousands of people from across this region will need to find longer-term housing. . . .

The federal government will undertake a close partnership with the states of Louisiana and Mississippi, the city of New Orleans, and other Gulf Coast cities, so they can rebuild in a sensible, well-planned way. Federal funds will cover the great majority of the costs of repairing public infrastructure in the disaster zone, from roads and bridges to schools and water systems. Our goal is to get the work done quickly. And taxpayers expect this work to be done honestly and wisely—so we'll have a team of inspectors general reviewing all expenditures.

In the rebuilding process, there will be many important decisions and many details to resolve, yet we're moving forward according to some clear principles. The federal government will be fully engaged in the mission, but Governor [Haley] Barbour, Governor [Kathleen] Blanco, Mayor [Ray] Nagin, and other state and local leaders will have the primary role in planning for their own future. Clearly, communities will need to move decisively to change zoning laws and building codes, in order to avoid a repeat of what we've seen. And in the work of rebuilding, as many jobs as possible should go to the men and women who live in Louisiana, Mississippi, and Alabama.

Our third commitment is this: When communities are rebuilt, they must be even better and stronger than before the storm. Within the Gulf region are some of the most beautiful and historic places in America. As all of us saw on television, there's also some deep, persistent poverty in this region, as well. That poverty has roots in a history of racial discrimination, which cut off generations from the opportunity of America. We have a duty to confront this poverty with bold action. So let us restore all that we have cherished from yesterday, and let us rise above the legacy of inequality. When the streets are rebuilt, there should be many new businesses, including minority-owned businesses, along those streets. When the houses are rebuilt, more families should own, not rent, those houses. When the regional economy revives, local people should be prepared for the jobs being created.

Americans want the Gulf Coast not just to survive, but to thrive; not just to cope, but to overcome. We want evacuees to come home, for the best of reasons—because they have a real chance at a better life in a place they love.

Three Initiatives for Rebuilding

The cash needed to support the armies of compassion is great, and Americans have given generously. When one resident of this city who lost his home was asked by a reporter if he would relocate, he said, "Naw, I will rebuild—but I will build higher." That is our vision for the future, in this city and beyond: We'll not just rebuild, we'll build higher and better. To meet this goal, I will listen to good ideas from Congress, and state and local officials, and the private sector. I believe we should start with three initiatives that the Congress should pass.

Tonight I propose the creation of a Gulf Opportunity Zone, encompassing the region of the disaster in Louisiana and Mississippi and Alabama. Within this zone, we should provide immediate incentives for job-creating investment, tax relief for

64

small businesses, incentives to companies that create jobs, and loans and loan guarantees for small businesses, including minority-owned enterprises, to get them up and running again. It is entrepreneurship that creates jobs and opportunity; it is entrepreneurship that helps break the cycle of poverty; and we will take the side of entrepreneurs as they lead the economic revival of the Gulf region.

I propose the creation of Worker Recovery Accounts to help those evacuees who need extra help finding work. Under this plan, the federal government would provide accounts of up to $5,000, which these evacuees could draw upon for job training and education to help them get a good job, and for child care expenses during their job search.

And to help lower-income citizens in the hurricane region build new and better lives, I also propose that Congress pass an Urban Homesteading Act. Under this approach, we will identify property in the region owned by the federal government, and provide building sites to low-income citizens free of charge, through a lottery. In return, they would pledge to build on the lot, with either a mortgage or help from a charitable organization like Habitat for Humanity. Home ownership is one of the great strengths of any community, and it must be a central part of our vision for the revival of this region.

> *Americans want the Gulf Coast not just to survive, but to thrive.*

In the long run, the New Orleans area has a particular challenge, because much of the city lies below sea level. The people who call it home need to have reassurance that their lives will be safer in the years to come. Protecting a city that sits lower than the water around it is not easy, but it can, and has been done. City and parish officials in New Orleans, and state officials in Louisiana will have a large part in the engineering decisions to come. And the Army Corps of Engineers will work at their side to make the flood protection system stronger than it has ever been.

The work that has begun in the Gulf Coast region will be one of the largest reconstruction efforts the world has ever seen. When that job is done, all Americans will have something to be very proud of—and all Americans are needed in this common effort. It is the armies of compassion—charities and houses of worship, and idealistic men and women—that give our reconstruction effort its humanity. They offer to those who hurt a friendly face, an arm around the shoulder, and the reassurance that in hard times, they can count on someone who cares. By land, by sea, and by air, good people wanting to make a difference deployed to the Gulf Coast, and they've been working around the clock ever since.

The cash needed to support the armies of compassion is great, and Americans have given generously. . . .

Examining the Government Response

The government of this nation will do its part, as well. Our cities must have clear and up-to-date plans for responding to natural disasters, and disease outbreaks, or a terrorist attack, for evacuating large numbers of people in an emergency, and for providing the food and water and security they would need. In a time of terror threats and weapons of mass destruction, the danger to our citizens reaches much wider than a fault line or a flood plain. I consider detailed emergency planning to be a national security priority, and therefore, I've ordered the Department of Homeland Security to undertake an immediate review, in cooperation with local counterparts, of emergency plans in every major city in America.

I also want to know all the facts about the government response to Hurricane Katrina. The storm involved a massive flood, a major supply and security operation, and an evacuation order affecting more than a million people. It was not a normal hurricane—and the normal disaster relief system was not equal to it. Many of the men and women of the Coast Guard, the Federal Emergency Management Agency, the United States military, the National Guard, Homeland Security, and state and local governments performed skillfully under the worst conditions. Yet the system, at every level of government, was not well-coordinated, and was overwhelmed in the first few days. It is now clear that a challenge on this scale requires greater federal authority and a broader role for the armed forces—the institution of our government most capable of massive logistical operations on a moment's notice.

Four years after the frightening experience of September the 11th, Americans have every right to expect a more effective response in a time of emergency. When the federal government fails to meet such an obligation, I, as President, am responsible for the problem, and for the solution. So I've ordered every Cabinet Secretary to participate in a comprehensive review of the government response to the hurricane. This government will learn the lessons of Hurricane Katrina. We're going to review every action and make necessary changes, so that we are better prepared for any challenge of nature, or act of evil men, that could threaten our people.

> *The cash needed to support the armies of compassion is great, and Americans have given generously.*

The United States Congress also has an important oversight function to perform. Congress is preparing an investigation, and I will work with members of both parties to make sure this effort is thorough.

Hope for the Future

In the life of this nation, we have often been reminded that nature is an awesome force, and that all life is fragile. We're the heirs of men and women who lived through those first terrible winters at Jamestown and Plymouth, who rebuilt Chicago after a great fire, and San Francisco after a great earthquake, who reclaimed the prairie from the Dust Bowl of the 1930s. Every time, the people of this land have come back from fire, flood, and storm to build anew—and to build better than what we had before. Americans have never left our destiny to the whims of nature—and we will not start now.

These trials have also reminded us that we are often stronger than we know—with the help of grace and one another. They remind us of a hope beyond all pain and death, a God who welcomes the lost to a house not made with hands. And they remind us that we're tied together in this life, in this nation—and that the despair of any touches us all.

I know that when you sit on the steps of a porch where a home once stood, or sleep on a cot in a crowded shelter, it is hard to imagine a bright future. But that future will come. The streets of Biloxi and Gulfport will again be filled with lovely homes and the sound of children playing. The churches of Alabama will have their broken steeples mended and their congregations whole. And here in New Orleans, the street cars will once again rumble down St. Charles, and the passionate soul of a great city will return.

In this place, there's a custom for the funerals of jazz musicians. The funeral procession parades slowly through the streets, followed by a band playing a mournful dirge as it moves to the cemetery. Once the casket has been laid in place, the band breaks into a joyful "second line"—symbolizing the triumph of the spirit over death. Tonight the Gulf Coast is still coming through the dirge—yet we will live to see the second line.

Thank you, and may God bless America.

13

Federal Government Spending on Hurricane Victims Should Be Limited

Duane D. Freese

Duane D. Freese is a journalist and writer.

Politicians, including President George W. Bush, have made extravagant promises to help victims and rebuild the Gulf region following Hurricane Katrina. However, care must be taken to ensure that such programs do not bankrupt the federal government or make it more difficult to help victims of future disasters. Programs aimed at discrete groups such as hurricane victims inevitably expand into expensive government programs that serve every community hit by a disaster or problem. The government should focus its efforts on infrastructure and on providing educational training and limited assistance to hurricane victims.

With apologies to [Isaac] Newton, every catastrophic action leads to a massive political and economic overreaction.

And with apologies to George Santayana, those politicians and bureaucrats who remember the lessons of history are doomed to have learned the wrong ones.

That certainly has been the case with Hurricane Katrina.

The outpouring of support for people in the Gulf region from every part of the country is heartening. And federal spend-

Duane D. Freese, "Will Katrina Impoverish the Nation?" *Tech Central Station*, September 19, 2005. Copyright © 2005 by *Tech Central Station*, www.techcentral station.com. Reproduced by permission.

ing to rebuild infrastructure is essential to the general economic health of the nation, even if it does temporarily increase federal spending. The *Wall Street Journal* quoted Ben Bernanke, chairman of the president's Council of Economic Advisers, "The costs of rebuilding after Katrina are, of course, substantial and will add to the budget deficit in the near term; incurring those costs is essential if we are to repair the unprecedented damage wrought by that natural disaster. This necessary spending should not, however, jeopardize the president's long-term deficit-reduction goals."

To repair and revive is one thing, though; to rebuild New Orleans better than it was, as President Bush promised . . . , or bring all the New Orleans residents back as Louisiana Gov. Kathleen Blanco vowed . . . , is something else.

Republican senators have sent a letter to the president calling for a Marshall Plan. Former House Speaker Newt Gingrich has suggested creating a new government-sponsored enterprise—a Gulf States Redevelopment Corp, backed by the federal government and regulated by regional officials, that would issue bonds and make loans for development and the levees. Jack Kemp, a former House member and head of the Department of Housing and Urban Development, has succeeded in pushing his long-championed enterprise zones idea, with Bush promising to create an Opportunity Zone for the gulf region.

A Question of Fairness

Everybody cares. But this outpouring of aid raises a big question of fairness—not to mention common sense in federal subsidies encouraging people to live below sea level in hurricane prone zones.

> *This outpouring of aid raises a big question of fairness.*

Already in Washington, D.C., homeless families and individuals who've waited in line for housing vouchers for months are being told they'll wait some more so aid can flow to the victims of Katrina.

Katrina victims will get $5,000 for training so they might

better their lives. Other poor people, not from hurricane-prone areas, pay for training themselves or remain stuck in low-paying jobs. To rectify this seeming injustice, some are calling for a massive expansion of vouchers and of training programs, all at taxpayer expense, to make sure no one is left out. As many of the poor are minorities, how can the president refuse them? After all, hasn't he admitted now that poverty among minorities is a legacy of discrimination, and doesn't the federal government, if it is going to relieve poverty of minorities in New Orleans have the same obligation in other places where poor minorities live? Are some poor more worthy due to location than others?

> *Grand strategies to rebuild New Orleans better than it was will only lead to every community seeking similar advantages.*

Helping the victims of Katrina is expensive enough, but it will quickly become unaffordable when the programs for New Orleans and the Gulf morph into programs to serve every other community with a problem.

How Government Programs Grow

That's what happened after the urban riots in the 1960s. Urban Development Action Grants aimed at revitalizing and improving inner cities were converted due to program failures into Community Development Block Grants for poor communities. And that morphed into programs to help poor sections in any community. The Government Accountability Office (formerly, the General Accounting Office) reported in 2000 that wealthy "Greenwich Connecticut received five times more funding per person in poverty in 1995 than that provided to Camden, New Jersey, even though Greenwich, with per capita income six times greater than Camden, could more easily afford its own community development needs."

As the National Academy of Sciences noted in a report in 1983, "Whatever the original reasons for these subsidies, they have often continued, almost as entitlements, without serious assessment of their impact on the flow of capital to other sectors that might improve both national economic efficiency and interregional or intergroup equity."

The complaint here? It's not that the victims of Katrina don't deserve help. But helping others in ways that are not limited in scope will make us less capable of helping victims in future catastrophes.

The federal government should focus its aid on individuals and on infrastructure with importance for interstate commerce and national defense. . . . And the government can help individuals receive training, through the network of community and private two-year colleges around the country.

Grand strategies to rebuild New Orleans better then it was will only lead to every community seeking similar advantages. And it will make the entire nation poorer.

14

New Orleans Should Not Be Rebuilt

Klaus Jacob

Klaus Jacob teaches disaster risk management at Columbia University's School of International and Public Affairs.

Hurricane Katrina was in many respects a disaster waiting to happen. New Orleans, in addition to existing in hurricane country, lies ten feet below sea level. Levees and dams are stopgap measures that will not prevent the area from total submersion in the next hundred years. New Orleans cannot be rebuilt as it was. The government should instead plan a careful deconstruction of New Orleans.

It is time to swim against the tide. The direction of public discourse in the wake of Katrina goes like this: First we save lives and provide some basic assistance to the victims. Then we clean up New Orleans. And then we rebuild the city. Most will rightly agree on the first two. But should we rebuild New Orleans, 10 feet below sea level, just so it can be wiped out again?

Some say we can raise and strengthen the levees to fully protect the city. Here is some unpleasant truth: The higher the defenses, the deeper the floods that will inevitably follow. The current political climate is not conducive to having scientific arguments heard before political decisions are made. But not doing so leads to the kind of chaos we are seeing now.

This is not a natural disaster. It is a social, political, human and—to a lesser degree—engineering disaster. To many experts, it is a disaster that was waiting to happen. In fact, Katrina is not even the worst-case scenario. Had the eye of the storm made landfall just west of the city (instead of to the east, as it did) the wind speeds and its associated coastal storm surge would have been higher in New Orleans (and lower in Gulfport, Miss.). The city would have flooded faster, and the loss of life would have been greater.

Geological Realities

What scientific facts do we need before making fateful political, social and economic decisions about New Orleans's future? Here are just two:

First, all river deltas tend to subside as fresh sediment (supplied during floods) compacts and is transformed into rock. The Mississippi River delta is no exception. In the early to mid-20th century, the Army Corps of Engineers was charged with protecting New Orleans from recurring natural floods. At the same time, the Corps kept the river (and some related canals) along defined pathways. These well-intended defensive measures prevented the natural transport of fresh sediments into the geologically subsiding areas. The protected land and the growing city sank, some of it to the point that it is now 10 feet below sea level. Over time, some of the defenses were raised and strengthened to keep up with land subsidence and to protect against river floods and storm surges. But the defenses were never designed to safeguard the city against a direct hit by a Category 5 hurricane (on the Saffir-Simpson scale) or a Category 4 hurricane making landfall just west of the city.

> *It is time to face up to some geological realities and start a carefully planned deconstruction of New Orleans.*

Second, global sea levels have risen less than a foot in the past century, and will rise one to three feet by the end of this century. Yes, there is uncertainty. But there is no doubt in the scientific community that the rise in global sea levels will accelerate.

What does this mean for New Orleans's future? Government officials and academic experts have said for years that in about 100 years, New Orleans may no longer exist. Period.

Planning the Deconstruction of New Orleans

It is time to face up to some geological realities and start a carefully planned deconstruction of New Orleans, assessing what can or needs to be preserved, or vertically raised and, if affordable, by how much. Some of New Orleans could be transformed into a "floating city" using platforms not unlike the oil platforms offshore, or, over the short term, into a city of boathouses, to allow floods to fill in the 'bowl' with fresh sediment.

If realized, this "American Venice" would still need protection from the worst of storms. Restoration of mangroves and wetlands between the coast and the city would need to be carefully planned and executed. Much engineering talent would have to go into anchoring the floating assets to prevent chaos during storms. As for oil production, refining and transshipment facilities, buffer zones would have to be established to protect them from the direct onslaught of coastal storm surges.

Many ancient coastal cities of great fame have disappeared or are now shells of their former grandeur. Parts of ancient Alexandria suffered from the subsidence of the Nile delta, and earthquakes and tsunamis toppled the city's famed lighthouse, one of the "Seven Wonders of the Ancient World."

It is time that quantitative, science-based risk assessment became a cornerstone of urban and coastal land-use planning to prevent such disasters from happening again. Politicians and others must not make hollow promises for a future, safe New Orleans. Ten feet below sea level and sinking is not safe. It is time to constructively deconstruct, not destructively reconstruct.

15

New Orleans
Must Be Rebuilt

George Friedman

George Friedman is the founder of Statfor, a private geopolitical and public policy intelligence firm. He also directed the Center for Geopolitical Studies at Louisiana State University.

The United States has historically depended on the city and port of New Orleans to handle agriculture and industrial commodities traveling up and down the Mississippi River. Hurricane Katrina has taken out New Orleans as effectively as a nuclear bomb. Port facilities were damaged, not destroyed, but they require a local workforce that after Hurricane Katrina became scattered across America. A paralyzed New Orleans will create a national economic crisis. Geopolitical realities dictate that the city and port of New Orleans must be quickly rebuilt in its present location.

The American political system was founded in Philadelphia, but the American nation was built on the vast farmlands that stretch from the Alleghenies to the Rockies. That farmland produced the wealth that funded American industrialization: it permitted the formation of a class of small landholders who, amazingly, could produce more than they could consume. They could sell their excess crops in the East and in Europe and save that money, which eventually became the founding capital of American industry.

But it was not the extraordinary land or the farmers and ranchers who alone set the process in motion. Rather, it was geography—the extraordinary system of rivers that flowed through

George Friedman, "The Ghost City," *New York Review of Books,* vol. 52, October 6, 2005. Copyright © 2005 by NYREV, Inc. Reproduced by permission.

the Midwest and allowed them to ship their surplus to the rest of the world. All of the rivers flowed into one—the Mississippi—and the Mississippi flowed to the ports in and around one city: New Orleans. It was in New Orleans that the barges from upstream were unloaded and their cargos stored, sold, and reloaded on oceangoing vessels. . . . New Orleans was, in many ways, the pivot of the American economy.

> *On Sunday, August 28, [2005,] nature took out New Orleans almost as surely as a nuclear strike.*

For that reason, the Battle of New Orleans in January 1815 was a key moment in American history. Even though the battle occurred after the War of 1812 was over, had the British taken New Orleans, we suspect they wouldn't have given it back. Without New Orleans, the entire Louisiana Purchase would have been valueless to the United States. Or, to state it more precisely, the British would control the region because the value of the Purchase was the land and the rivers—which all converged on the Mississippi and the ultimate port of New Orleans. The hero of the battle was Andrew Jackson, and when he became president, his obsession with Texas had much to do with keeping the Mexicans away from New Orleans.

During the cold war, a macabre topic of discussion among bored graduate students who studied such things was this: If the Soviets could destroy one city with a large nuclear device, which would it be? The usual answers were Washington or New York. For me, the answer was simple: New Orleans. If the Mississippi River was shut to traffic, then the foundations of the economy would be shattered. The industrial minerals needed in the factories wouldn't come in, and the agricultural wealth wouldn't flow out. Alternative routes really weren't available. The Germans knew it too: a U-boat campaign occurred near the mouth of the Mississippi during World War II. New Orleans was the prize.

Hurricane Katrina Takes Out the Ports

On Sunday, August 28, [2005,] nature took out New Orleans almost as surely as a nuclear strike. Hurricane Katrina's geopolitical effect was not, in many ways, distinguishable from a mush-room cloud. The key exit from North America was closed. The petrochemical industry, which has become an added value to the region since Jackson's days, was at risk. The navigability of the Mississippi south of New Orleans was a question mark. New Orleans as a city and as a port complex had ceased to exist, and it was not clear that it could recover.

The ports of South Louisiana (POSL) and New Orleans, which run north and south of the city, are as important today as at any point during the history of the republic. On its own merit, POSL is the largest port in the United States by tonnage and the fifth-largest in the world. It exports more than 52 million tons a year, of which more than half are agricultural products—corn, soybeans, and so on. A large proportion of US agriculture flows out of the port. Even more cargo, nearly 69 million tons, comes in through the port—including not only crude oil, but chemicals and fertilizers, coal, concrete, and so on.

A simple way to think about the New Orleans port complex is that it is where the bulk commodities of American agriculture go out to the world and the bulk commodities needed for American industrialism come in. The commodity chain of the global food industry starts here, as does that of American industrialism. If these facilities are gone, more than the price of goods shifts: the very physical structure of the global economy would have to be reshaped. Consider the impact on the US auto industry if steel doesn't come up the river, or the effect on global food supplies if US corn and soybeans don't get to the markets.

The Shipping Issue

The problem is that there are no good shipping alternatives. River transport is cheap, and most of the commodities we are discussing have low value-to-weight ratios. The US transport system was built on the assumption that these commodities would travel to and from New Orleans by barge, where they would be loaded on ships or offloaded. Apart from port capacity elsewhere in the United States, there aren't enough trucks or rail cars to handle the long-distance hauling of these enormous quantities—assuming for the moment that the economics could be managed, which they can't be.

The focus in the press and television has been on the oil industry in Louisiana and Mississippi. This is not a trivial question, but in a certain sense it is dwarfed by the shipping issue.

First, Louisiana is the source of about 15 percent of US-produced petroleum, much of it from the Gulf. The local refineries are critical to American infrastructure. Were all of these facilities to be lost, the effect on the price of oil worldwide would be extraordinarily painful. If the river itself became unnavigable or if the ports are no longer functioning, however, the impact to the wider economy would be significantly more severe. In a sense, there is more flexibility in oil than in the physical transport of these other commodities.

> *Unlike in other disasters, [the New Orleans] workforce cannot return to the region because they have no place to live.*

There is clearly good news as information comes in. The Louisiana Offshore Oil Port, which services supertankers in the Gulf, suffered minimal damage while Port Fourchon, which serves it, has had no damage that could not readily be repaired. Offshore oil platforms have been damaged but, on the whole, they and the oil transportation network have generally held up.

The news on the river is also far better than might have been expected. The levees on the Mississippi continue to contain the river, which has not changed its course. The levees that broke and allowed water to pour into New Orleans were on the canal side and more weakly constructed. The Mississippi has not silted up and, while the Coast Guard continues to survey the river, it appears to be fully navigable. Even the port facilities, although obviously suffering some damage, are still there. The river as a transport corridor has not been lost.

A Lost City

What has been lost is the city of New Orleans and many of the residential suburbs around it. As I write, most of the population has fled, leaving behind a small number of people in desperate straits. Some are dead, others are dying, and the magnitude of the situation dwarfed the inadequate resources that were made available to relieve the condition of those who were trapped. But it is not the population that is still in and around New Orleans that is of geopolitical significance: it is the population that has left and has nowhere to return to.

The oil fields, pipelines, and ports required a skilled work-force in order to operate. That workforce requires homes. They require stores to buy food and other supplies. Hospitals and doctors. Schools for their children. In other words, in order to operate the facilities critical to the United States, you need a workforce to do it—and that workforce is gone. Unlike in other disasters, that workforce cannot return to the region because they have no place to live. New Orleans is gone, and the metropolitan area surrounding New Orleans is either gone or so badly damaged that most of it will not be habitable for a long time.

It may be possible to jury-rig around this problem for a short time. But the fact is that most of those who have left the area have gone to live with relatives and friends, or are in shelters far from New Orleans. Many also had networks of relationships and resources to manage their exile. But those resources are not infinite—and as it becomes apparent that these people will not be returning to New Orleans anytime soon, they will be enrolling their children in new schools, finding new jobs, finding new accommodations. If they have any insurance money coming, they will collect it. If they have none, then whatever emotional connections they may have to their home, their economic connection to it has been severed. In a very short time, these people will be making decisions that will start to reshape population and workforce patterns in the region.

> *The largest port in the United States cannot function without a city around it.*

A city is a complex and ongoing process—one that requires physical infrastructure to support the people who live in it and people to operate that physical infrastructure. I don't simply mean power plants and sewage treatment facilities, although they are critical. Someone has to be able to sell a bottle of milk or a new shirt. Someone has to be able to repair a car or do surgery. And the people who do those things, along with the infrastructure that supports them, are for the most part gone—and they are not coming back anytime soon.

It is in this sense, then, that it seems almost as if a nuclear weapon went off in New Orleans. The people mostly have fled rather than died, but they are gone. Not all of the facilities are destroyed, but most are. It appears to me that New Orleans and its environs have passed the point of recoverability. The area can recover, to be sure, but only with the commitment of huge resources from outside—and those resources would always be at risk to another Katrina.

> **❝** New Orleans is not optional for the United States' commercial infrastructure. **❞**

The displacement of population due to destruction, disease, and pollution is the crisis that New Orleans faces. It is also a national crisis, because the largest port in the United States cannot function without a city around it. The physical and business processes of a port cannot occur in a ghost town, and right now, except for the remaining refugees, that is what New Orleans is. It is not about the facilities, and it is not about the oil. It is about the loss of a city's population and the paralysis of the largest port in the United States.

New Orleans Must Return

Let's go back to the beginning. The United States historically has depended on the Mississippi and its tributaries for transport. Barges navigate the river. Ships go on the ocean. The barges must offload to the ships and vice versa. There must be a facility to make this exchange possible. It is also the facility where goods are stored in transit. Without this port, the river can't be used. Protecting that port has been, from the time of the Louisiana Purchase, a fundamental national security issue for the United States.

Katrina and the events following it have taken out the port—not by fatally destroying the facilities, but by rendering the area uninhabited and potentially uninhabitable. That means that even if the Mississippi remains navigable, the absence of a port near the mouth of the river makes the Mississippi enormously less useful than it was. For these reasons, the United States has lost not only its biggest port complex, but also the utility of its river transport system—the foundation of the entire American transport system. There are some substitutes, but none with sufficient capacity to solve the problem.

It follows from this that the port will have to be revived and, one would assume, at least some part of the city as well. The ports around New Orleans are located as far north as they can be while still being accessible to oceangoing vessels. The need for ships to be able to pass each other in the waterways, which narrow to the north, adds to the problem. Besides, the Highway 190 bridge in Baton Rouge blocks the river going north for oceangoing vessels. Barges can pass under the bridge, but cargo must first be transferred to them, and for that a port is needed. New Orleans is where it is for a reason: the United States needs a city right there.

New Orleans is not optional for the United States' commercial infrastructure. Vulnerable to inundation, it is a terrible place for a city to be located, but exactly the place where a city must exist. With that as a given, a city of some kind will return there because the alternatives are too devastating. The harvest is coming, and that means that the port, or part of it, will have to be opened soon. The port area will have to be cleared, by herculean effort if necessary. As in Iraq, premiums will be paid to people prepared to endure the hardships of working in New Orleans. But in the end, the city will return because it has to.

Geopolitics concerns permanent geographical realities and the way they interact with political life. If the logic of geopolitics prevails, it will force the city's resurrection, even if it will be greatly changed, and in the worst imaginable place.

Organizations to Contact

American Red Cross
2025 E St. NW, Washington, DC 20006
(202) 303-4498
Web site: www.redcross.org

The American Red Cross is a volunteer-led humanitarian organization that works to provide relief to disaster victims and help people prepare for and respond to emergencies. It publishes and distributes brochures, videos, and other materials related to disaster preparedness, including *Facing Fear: Helping Young People Deal with Terrorism and Tragic Events.* Information on its work for victims of Hurricane Katrina and other disasters can be found on its Web site.

Cato Institute
1000 Massachusetts Ave. NW, Washington, DC 20001-5403
(202) 842-0200 • fax: (202) 842-3490
e-mail: cato@cato.org • Web site: www.cato.org

Cato is a libertarian public policy research institute. It opposes a strong federal government role in all areas, including the environment and disaster preparedness and response. It publishes the quarterly magazine *Regulation* and the policy report *Did Big Government Return with Katrina?*

Economic Policy Institute (EPI)
1660 L St. NW, Suite 1200, Washington, DC 20036
(202) 775-8810 • fax: (202)775-0819
e-mail: epi@epi.org • Web site: www.epi.org

The Economic Policy Institute conducts research and promotes education programs on economic policy issues, particularly the economics of poverty, unemployment, and American industry. It supports organized labor and believes that government should invest in infrastructure and education to improve America's economy. Its publications include the briefing paper *Lessons for Post-Katrina Reconstruction* as well as other reports and studies.

Federal Emergency Management Agency (FEMA)
500 C St. SW, Washington, DC 20472
(800) 621-3362
e-mail: FEMAOPA@dhs.gov • Web site: www.fema.gov

The Federal Emergency Management Agency, a formerly independent government agency that became part of the Department of Homeland Security in March 2003, is tasked with responding to, planning for, recovering from, and mitigating disasters. Information on its programs and on natural disasters can be found on its Web site.

National Climatic Data Center (NCDC)
151 Patton Ave., Asheville, NC 28801-5001
(828) 271-4800 • fax: (828) 271-4876
e-mail: ncdc.info@noaa.gov • Web site: www.ncdc.noaa.gov

The NCDC is a federal government agency with the mission to track and analyze the nation's climate and weather patterns. Its Web site includes the world's largest archive of weather data, including details on all significant hurricanes in the United States since 1900. It publishes a quarterly newsletter.

National Hurricane Center (NHC)
11691 Seventeenth St. SW, Miami, Florida, 33165-2149
e-mail: nhc.public.affairs@noaa.gov • Web site: www.nhc.noaa.gov

The center maintains a continuous watch on tropical cyclones and prepares advisories and hurricane warnings for the public. Its Web site provides information on hurricane history and hurricane research.

National Oceanic and Atmospheric Administration (NOAA)
Fourteenth St. & Constitution Ave. NW, Room 6217
Washington, DC 20230
(202) 482-6090 • fax: (202) 482-3154
e-mail: answers@noaa.gov • Web site: www.noaa.gov

The NOAA provides general information on hurricanes. Its Web site provides links to participating agencies and information sources.

National Urban League (NUL)
120 Wall St., 8th Floor, New York, NY 10005
(212) 558-5300
e-mail: info@nul.org • Web site: www.nul.org

A community service agency, the National Urban League aims to eliminate institutional racism in the United States. It also provides services for minorities who experience discrimination in employment, housing, welfare, and other areas. The organization has been heavily involved in efforts to help Hurricane Katrina victims and rebuild New Orleans and other communities. It publishes the *Opportunity Journal* and the annual *State of Black America*.

United States Army Corps of Engineers (USACE)
441 G St. NW, Washington, DC 20314-1000
(202) 761-0011
Web site: www.usace.army.mil

The USACE plans and designs water resources and other civil works projects, including flood control. The corps operates and maintains 25,000 miles of navigable channels and is responsible for ports and waterways in forty-one states, including Louisiana and Mississippi. Its publications include the brochure *Deep Water Ports and Harbors* and news releases on its disaster response projects in areas hit by Hurricane Katrina, which are available on its Web site.

Worldwatch Institute
1776 Massachusetts Ave. NW, Washington, DC 20036-1904
(202) 452-1999 • fax: (202) 296-7368
e-mail: worldwatch@worldwatch.org • Web site: www.worldwatch.org

Worldwatch is a nonprofit public policy research organization dedicated to informing policymakers and the public about emerging global problems and trends. It publishes the bimonthly *World Watch* magazine, the Environmental Alert series, and several policy papers, including "Unnatural Disaster: The Lessons of Katrina." Recent and archived issues of *World Watch* are available on its Web site.

Bibliography

Books

John M. Barry	*Rising Tide: The Great Mississippi Flood of 1927 and How It Changed America.* New York: Simon & Schuster, 1998.
D.M. Brown	*Hurricane Katrina: The First Seven Days of America's Worst Natural Disaster.* Morrisville, NC: Lulu Press, 2005.
Pete Davies	*Inside the Hurricane: Face to Face with Nature's Deadliest Storms.* New York: Henry Holt, 2000.
Patrick J. Fitzpatrick	*Natural Disasters, Hurricanes: A Reference Handbook.* Santa Barbara, CA: ABC-CLIO, 1999.
Susan M. Moyer, ed.	*Hurricane Katrina: Stories of Rescue, Recovery, and Rebuilding in the Eye of the Storm.* New York: Spotlight Press, 2005.
Andrew Robinson	*Earthshock: Hurricanes, Volcanoes, Earthquakes, Tornadoes, and Other Forces of Nature.* New York: Thames & Hudson, 2002.
Bob Sheets and Jack Williams	*Hurricane Watch: Forecasting the Deadliest Storms on Earth.* New York: Vintage Books, 2001.
United States Government	*2005 Complete Guide to the Hurricane Katrina Disaster—Federal Reports, Government Response, Science Reports, Devastation to Louisiana, New Orleans, Mississippi, Alabama (DVD-ROM).* Mt. Laurel, NJ: Progressive Management, 2005.
Mary E. Williams, ed.	*Hurricanes.* San Diego: Greenhaven Press, 2004.

Periodicals

Julian E. Barnes and Kenneth T. Walsh	"A Uniform Response?" *U.S. News & World Report,* October 3, 2005.
Anna Bernasek	"Blueprints from Cities That Rose from Their Ashes," *New York Times,* October 9, 2005.
Carrie Black	"Six Reasons We Lost New Orleans: Environmental Degradation Made Katrina Much Worse," *Earth Island Journal,* Winter 2006.
Donna Brazile	"Don't Give In to Katrina Fatigue: There Are Still Millions of Gulf Coast Americans Who Need Our Help," *Time,* November 28, 2005.

Richard A. Clarke   "Things Left Undone: Why Has an Administration That Talks So Much About Homeland Security Been So Unable to Secure the Homeland?" *Atlantic Monthly*, November 2005.

Carrie Coolidge   "Insuring Against Mother Nature," *Forbes*, December 12, 2005.

Jason Deparle   "Liberal Hopes Ebb in Post-Storm Poverty Debate," *New York Times*, October 11, 2005.

Brian Duffy et al.   "Anatomy of a Disaster: 5 Days That Changed a Nation," *U.S. News & World Report*. September 26, 2005.

Daniel Eisenberg et al.   "The Displaced: Which Way Is Home?" *Time*, November 28, 2005.

Andrew J. Glass   "The Katrina Effect," *New Leader*, September/October 2005.

Terry Golway   "A Lesson in Perspective," *America*, October 3, 2005.

Jeffrey J. Guhin   "Katrina's Rainbow," *America*, September 26, 2005.

Carl Hoffmann   "The Kindness of Strangers," *Popular Mechanics*, December 2005.

Michael Ignatieff   "The Broken Contract," *New York Times Magazine*, September 25, 2005.

Naomi Klein   "Needed: A People's Reconstruction," *Nation*, September 26, 2005.

Nicholas Lemann   "In the Ruins," *New Yorker*, September 12, 2005.

Eric Lipton   "A View of the Political Storm After Katrina," *New York Times,* December 4, 2005.

John McWhorter   "'Racism!' They Charged: When Don't They?" *National Review*, September 26, 2005.

National Review   "The Blame Game," September 26, 2005.

New Scientist   "Flawed Levees No Match for Katrina," November 12, 2005.

Karol Dewulf Nickell   "1716 Locust," *Better Homes and Gardens*, December 2005.

Nicholas Ouroussoff   "How the City Sank," *New York Times*, October 9, 2005.

Christine Parenti   "The Big Easy Dies Hard," *Nation*, September 26, 2005.

Kathleen Pender   "The True Cost of Katrina," *San Francisco Chronicle*, September 27, 2005.

Virginia Postrel   "When Disasters Act as Accelerators of Change," *New York Times*, October 6, 2005.

David Remnick   "Under Water," *New Yorker*, September 12, 2005.

Daniel Schorr   "Katrina from Abroad," *New Leader*, September/
                       October 2005.

David Sirota   "Welcome to New Orleans," *In These Times*, Octo-
                       ber 24, 2001.

Annalyn Swan   "Out of the Rubble . . . Condos and Slots? We Will
                       Never Re-Create the Biloxi I Loved as a Child, but
                       We Must Try to Build Something Just as Unique,"
                       Newsweek, October 3, 2005.

Marianne   "Shattered Lives," *U.S. News & World Report*,
Szegedy-Maszak   October 3, 2005.

Cathy Booth Thomas   "New Orleans Today: It's Worse than You Think,"
et al.   *Time*, November 28, 2005.

Mike Tidwell   "Giving Up on New Orleans," *Los Angeles Times*,
                       December 6, 2005.

Steven Yates   "Expanding Federal Power: The Real Lessons of
                       Hurricane Katrina: New Government Programs
                       Mean Expanded Federal Powers and Increased
                       Dependence on Government," *New American*,
                       November 14, 2005.

Index

88